535 NOT I

DICK GEPHARDT

with KEN GRANT

"Having worked with Dick for over 20 years in Congress, I hope many will read his fascinating book and learn why democracy often fails and moves slowly and haltingly but ultimately is far superior to other forms of human governance."

— TOM DASCHLE, Former Democratic Member of Congress, Democratic Leader, U.S. Senate

"Dick Gephardt's public career was always about figuring out how to make democracy work for the American people. He was enormously respected by both sides of the aisle, and his bipartisan efforts should be a template for today's politicians. I had a unique opportunity to observe his talents and sincerity when he served as a director of Ford Motor Company's board."

— BILL FORD, Executive Chairman of Ford Motor Company

"While our democratic republic can sometimes seem messy and polarizing, history has shown that the autocratic alternatives can have devastating consequences. No leader in the past 50 years has been more adept at navigating the legislative process in Congress to reach bipartisan solutions on our nation's toughest problems than Dick Gephardt. Dick's incomparable ability to bring people with different opinions together on critical issues has established him as a leader in politics and the private sector, where I have been proud to serve with him on the Spirit AeroSystems Board of Directors for the past 6 years. His new book, "535 Not 1," provides a roadmap for how we can leverage his accumulated lessons to continue building a brighter future for us all."

— TOM GENTILE, CEO and President, Spirit AeroSystems

"Our most important challenge in these perilous times is protecting our democracy. Dick Gephardt's insightful book allows readers to better understand how our democracy actually works and why, with all of its faults, it is far superior to the alternative."

— WALTER ISAACSON, American Author, Journalist, and Professor

"In his many years of public service, Dick Gephardt's great gift was his ability to bring people together. Members of Congress looked to him for the sane center, the moderate middle. As he puts it in this book, "The real strength of humans is in our ability to communicate, share ideas, and collaborate solutions." Dick Gephardt made this an art form while he was our extraordinary Leader in Congress. Today, as so many of us are frustrated by our current system, simply put, we need more Dick Gephardts."

— MARJORIE MARGOLIES, President of Women's Campaign International, former Democratic Member of Congress

"My friend and colleague's personal reflections are a timely and powerful reminder of the wisdom and foresight of our Founding Fathers in rejecting authoritarian rule as they designed the constitutional framework of our Republic."

— TOM RIDGE, Former Republican of Congress, Governor of Pennsylvania, and first Leader of Department of Homeland Security

Print ISBN: 978-1-66784-965-2
eBook ISBN: 978-1-66784-966-9

cover design credit (Ian Webb)

INTRODUCTION

On September 17, 1787, 39 of the 55 delegates to the Constitutional Convention signed and approved the compromise that was the U.S. Constitution. The U.S. Constitution embodied a very radical idea: that four million U.S. citizens could govern themselves by diffusing the power of their governance to elected representatives rather than giving that power to one human being.

Before the experiment was launched in 1787, no other country in the world had attempted this. In 1787, the first Congress met in New York City with eight of the 22 new members of the Senate and with 13 of the 65 members of the U.S. House who could attend.

I wrote this book to give readers a sense as to what it was like to be one member of the Congress 200 years after this grand experiment was launched — and when the group size had become 535 representing 220 million Americans (U.S. population in 1977 when I arrived in Congress) — instead of 87 people representing four million Americans.

In telling my story, I wish to convey an overriding theme: the political process with its flaws, inefficiencies, shortcomings, and attendant frustrations is the best and perhaps the only effective antidote to what happens in the absence of the democratically established rule of law: government by violence.

We can either have process that allows for governance under which everyone has a voice in reaching a compromise, or we can allow one person to singlehandedly make all the decisions on behalf of the entire country.

Those that advocate rule by force are always out there, seeking to achieve control over others. Unless society perpetually recommits to the political process, the seekers of unilateral power are likely to win the day. However, even when an authoritarian gains control to rule by violence, they are constantly under the risk of removal by popular will and revolution.

Throughout the past 250 years, society has debated this topic and continues to do so to this day. The myriad advantages of democracy over authoritarian modes of government are abundantly clear.

In his landmark book, "Democracy as Freedom" (Anchor, 1999), Nobel Economics Laureate (1998) Amartya Sen wrote: "No famine has ever taken place in the history of the world in a functioning democracy." And while the precise statement can be justifiably debated (the Irish Potato Famine of the nineteenth century comes to mind as a counterexample), it is, in essence, correct. Across history, where democratically elected citizens form effective governing bodies, famine, homelessness, abject poverty, genocide, and other scourges are the rare exception — particularly in the modern world of resources available in sufficient abundance to feed, clothe, and provide medicine and shelter to its population. By contrast, societies that are either ruled by mobs or dictators experience these sufferings routinely.

Moreover, one does not need to look back into history to note the contrast. In Western societies, almost no one starves and only a very small percentage of the population endures homelessness. Means and methods exist to shelter and feed the poor and care for the sick.

Admittedly, our execution and distribution of these blessings is far from perfect and, in fact, desperately and perpetually needs improvement. But I urge you to compare our conduct in these areas to that of democracy-bereft nations like Darfur, North Korea, Haiti, and Venezuela where all manner of the human sufferings catalogued above are routine elements of daily living.

I believe that self-government — with the rule of law at its foundation — provides better nutrition, shelter, and overall economic benefit due to its superiority as a model for the distribution of goods and services and human governance.

At the end of the day, authoritarian governments are always less competent than democracies because all decisions are made by one person. The real strength of humans is our ability to communicate, share ideas, and collaborate on solutions. As difficult and complicated as that process often is, it is superior to one person making decisions for everyone else. That consensus process produces less corruption and the ability to correct mistakes or foolish decisions made in the past.

In authoritarian models, individual citizens are less motivated to engage in the practice of starting and participating in business. In these types of societies, the country's leaders claim most of the economic wealth because they control the economy. We do not need to look any further than current data on annual per capita income in authoritarian-run countries compared with democracies. Here are a few recent examples (2021 data):

- Russia $12,000 compared to Taiwan $33,000
- Venezuela $3,400 compared to Canada $52,000
- North Korea $1,700 compared to South Korea $34,000

Across more than fifty years in and around politics, I have witnessed firsthand the blessings and shortcomings of the political process. As some readers may be aware, I was born into what only can be described as humble conditions. My father was a milkman; my mother a housewife. Through hard, honest work, they provided me with the means to achieve my ambitions (well, most of them, anyway) and also set the example I needed to reach these goals. I entered politics at a young age, not long after having graduated from University of Michigan Law School.

I did multiple tours of duty in the Air Force National Guard and served for five years as Alderman for the City of St. Louis. In 1976, I ran for U.S. Congress in Missouri's Third Congressional District and won. I was re-elected to the House 13 times. I ran for the Democratic Party's nomination for President twice and lost both times. I served as House Majority Leader for over five years — from June 1989 until January 1995 — when my party ceded control of Congress to the Republicans after the 1994 mid-term election. I continued to serve my district and the country for another five terms (ten years) as House Minority Leader. I retired from that great legislative body at the end of 2004.

Through it all, I witnessed — in fact participated in — the glories and failings of the democratic process through some great triumphs and several important episodes of failure. Across these experiences, I learned virtually everything there is to know about how the system works. Indisputably, it is chockful of deceit, self-dealing, hypocrisy, and virtually all the Seven Deadly Sins that pre-date even Greek teachings. However, though seldom appropriately celebrated, it is also graced with the Seven Heavenly Virtues contained in the Catechism, particularly Charity, Diligence, Patience, Kindness, and Humility. The glorious, near 250-year American Experience, proves this to be so.

As we will re-tell in these pages, I have participated in political processes that often and at the time seemed quixotic and intractable. Both sides dig in, both are playing to specific constituencies, both feel that victory is essential — not only from a policy perspective but also for their own political well-being and advancement. Eventually, the most sublime political power of them all — the will of the people — forces them to the negotiating table. There is give and take, tempers flare, and frustrations reach a boiling point, but, inexorably, the dynamic moves toward compromise. Nobody gets exactly what they want. Everybody is forced to sacrifice some Sacred Cows, but a deal is ultimately reached and the business of the nation moves forward. Take my word for it: the process, when viewed with the benefit of retrospect and context, is always a "God-damned mess," but it is at the same time nothing short of divine.

Throughout our history, when self-government wanes — either because the compromise decisions produced are so abhorrent to large numbers of citizens or citizens feel the decision-making process is unfair — people turn to violence.

Our Civil War in the 1860s is a prime example, but there are other, smaller, similar episodes that reinforce the point. The civil unrest of the 1960s illustrates the realities of political processes failing to offer effective substitutes to violence. However, when politics wins the day, and big, divisive issues are settled through compromise, the result is sublime. I observed many examples of this — processes that left large numbers of citizens frustrated, angry, and on the verge of violence. But, because they perceived the resolution process to be fair, they were grudgingly willing to accept the decision. They didn't leave the country and were able to live with the outcome because they felt their voices were heard. If they felt strongly about an issue, they bided their time until it was ripe to fight for their points of view again.

I view these touchpoints of history as reinforcing the core tenet of this book. Absent ordinary citizens having an opportunity to be heard through the political process, we risk dictatorship. It is largely for this reason that I have devoted my life to the nurturing and cultivation of the political process. In any number of situations, I've experienced success and failure with respect to my specific policy objectives, but across it all I continue to revere the process.

Across these pages, I hope to reinforce this essential point: politics plays a critical role in the health and well-being of the human race. And I will attempt to show this through both positive and negative examples.

Additionally, it would be illogical to cover these topics without reference to the current political and social context. The point in history in which I am writing is generally viewed as one of the greatest eras of domestic political strife, possibly since the late 1960s period referenced above. One might even argue that our two political parties and American citizens are at odds with one another at levels not experienced since 1860. A vast majority of Americans polled are dissatisfied both with the government as it is now comprised and at the direction in which they believe the United States is headed.

Given what is at stake, and to borrow a phrase typically attributed to Apollo 13 Flight Director Gene Kranz (immortalized in the eponymous Ron Howard and Tom Hanks film): "Failure is not an option."

The critical nature of politically driven governance is a topic that has fascinated me for my entire life. And, as is the case with so many aspects of our existence, I find that its development follows an evolutionary trajectory. Laying aside the eternal question as to whether humanity was spawned by Adam and Eve in the Garden of Eden or, alternatively, crawled in reptilian fashion out of the primordial ooze, what has transpired subsequently can be described with a measure of accuracy. We are indeed descended from the same genetic pool as chimpanzees and then evolved into hominids (pre-humans).

Our evolution continued and this evoked the need for the development of social constructs. Many thousands of years ago, social mankind first formed itself in tribal fashion, with each tribe being comprised of between thirty and fifty members. To survive, living in a world where physical threats were perpetual (extreme weather, food shortages, disease, attacks from humans or other species), the qualities needed for survival were strength, courage, and will.

Naturally and logically, these groups were typically overseen by some alpha leader — the strongest, most willful, and most courageous of the clan — who made all decisions and imposed them upon his fellows by force if necessary. In subhuman species, this construct still dominates. Think of the lead wolf in wolf packs, or the rooster who fights his way to the top of the dunghill. Across this entire interval of history, and perhaps inevitably, "might makes right" was the dominant governance paradigm.

But, with respect to the human race — and perhaps as pre-ordained by God — both the species and its social forms experienced a period of rapid evolution. Our brain power expanded, leading to such paradigm shifts as the development of language and other forms of communication. Our numbers increased in dramatic fashion and began to dominate the geographic landscape of the planet. Humans figured out that cooperation, collaboration, and division of labor would enable the group to better protect itself against nature's hazards (and other stronger species) and avail itself more thoroughly of its bounty.

This led to the creation of villages, roads, common shelters, agriculture, and eventually socially critical developments such as medical facilities and schools.

Throughout, the specter of managing human interaction through physical power was ever-present and remains so to the present day. But, over the course of the centuries, a miracle of political process began to emerge. Early forms of this date back more than 5,000 years to the first societies formed in the Fertile Crescent at the intersection of the Tigris and Euphrates and have evolved dramatically in the ensuing five millennia. Much of course is due and owing to history's great empires — most notably, the Ancient Greeks, their Roman successors, and eventually the British Empire — which created the Common Law upon which modern jurisprudence is based. However, for our purposes, we will use the formation of the United States as origin of reference for the development of modern political processes, and its magnificent over-riding governing document — the United States Constitution — as the genesis of our journey.

Irrespective of this, one thing is clear: when societies migrate from tribal constructs to integrated socioeconomic mechanisms, the leadership qualities needed to achieve social objectives morph from strength, will, and ambition, into the more civilized traits of empathy, cooperation, collaboration, and sacrifice. Note that the former set of behaviors is still present and abundant, but history has repeatedly demonstrated that wherever the latter, more nurturing traits prevail in a government, the better off the society is.

Notably, the needs and nature of government processes have evolved along with other forms of human interaction. Governments began through the development of city-states, and though these societies were largely ruled by military might, they formed broad contours of what we now think of as modern democratic governance. Populations were, of course, much smaller back then. At the peak of its powers around the period of the Peloponnesian Wars, the city of Athens — perhaps the most prominent of the ancient nation-states — numbered less than 700,000 (smaller than that of Baltimore, MD). Yes, there was a form of democracy featuring the aforementioned Heavenly Virtues, but franchise was exceedingly limited, and overall, its governance was perhaps best described as a hybrid between the violent dictatorship and democracy paradigms.

Over time, populations grew, as did geographic reach, and nation-states became nations — a process that compelled the formation of hierarchical governing structures such as that upon which this country was founded. Today, virtually every major democratic nation is divided into states or provinces and municipalities — each with its own government construct — that interact with central governments to form the delicate dance of modern democracy.

And the process of growth and complexity continues. During the span of my lifetime, global population has grown from approximately three billion to nearly eight billion, and by mid-century could reach ten billion. At each rung on this ladder, given the finite resources of the world (as well as the critical need to preserve them that will be a major sub-theme of this document), the complexity of democratic governance will become more complicated by orders of magnitude. Though difficult to quantify, there is most certainly a natural limit to the number of individuals that can fit into a single system of governance by consent of the governed. The contemporaneous challenges of managing our affairs in a fragile world, featuring a growing population, unmistakable threats to the environment, and myriad other issues will be the most important issue for the next generation.

Further, and as will be discussed in more detail in subsequent chapters, the above is transpiring against a rapidly changing, technology-driven telecommunications environment that creates instantaneous touchpoints between virtually everyone in the world. Even in regions rife with hunger, disease, and abject poverty, vast majorities of the population own smart phones. Among many far-flung implications of this trend, not only is information (factual and otherwise) distributed in previously unimaginable magnitude and speed, but so too is opinion.

The implications, for what is generically described as journalism, are beyond profound; in fact, a strong argument can be made that journalism as we have come to know it no longer exists.

Over the course of my adult life, I've witnessed the migration from a world where citizens got their news and formed their opinions from a finite roster of newspapers, magazines, and televised network news, to one that first was overtaken by cable news outlets. Now it is being strongly supplemented by the algorithmic behavior of social media platforms that boost information to users that make them angry and anxious that maintains their attention on the platform. The net result is that the platforms increase profitability and the users are in a heightened state of anxiety.

Citizens have no way of judging whether the "facts" are true and balanced, somewhat true, or not true at all. Thus, there are no shared facts. The worst result is that this information culture creates bitter division and polarization of the American people. As Lincoln said, "A house divided against itself cannot stand."

It follows, additionally, that if our nation is bitterly divided, so will its representative bodies (i.e., Congress) because Congress is a reflection of the American people. Taken to an extreme, we stand to lose our democratic system as we nearly did in the 1860s. Failure is NOT an option.

Challenges will continue. The world's resources will become increasingly constrained. The environment will suffer myriad assaults from the activities of mankind. Information and advocacy will flow at a faster and more furious pace. Human beings will have no alternative other than to shoulder on and do the best they can — for themselves, their families, their communities, their country, and our species. If our democracy fails, none of these challenges can be successfully met.

For me, there is an answer right there in front of us: the miracle of the democratic process. While it has, from its outset and to this day, been under perpetual attack, it has endured and thrived. In 1910, approximately 10 percent of the world lived under what can truly be called democratic systems of governance. Today — a little over a century later — the share has risen to roughly 60 percent. Yes, there is pushback, and, as has been the case throughout history, a portion of the world risks slipping back into authoritarianism and rule by violence. Simply, we cannot allow this to happen.

But the process is difficult. In the United States, more than 300 million residents elect 535 legislators (100 Senators and 435 Members of Congress) to create laws on their behalf that reflect the best interests of the multitudes. This is a miraculous blessing bestowed upon us by our founders. Prior to the implementation of their vision, even where representative governments existed, they were selected by the *privileged* classes for the unilateral benefit of the privileged classes. Here and now — in this time and space — everyone has a voice. If we can simply abide by this principle, we can continue to avoid disaster and reach even greater heights.

I hope that by telling my story I can in some small way further this thinking. I was first elected to Congress in 1976, replacing a twelve-term incumbent. Every two years in our 240-year history, the American people decide who will make decisions for them and their families. In 1976, the American electorate — frustrated and fed up with a Washington power core that had brought us the Vietnam War, Watergate, and the subsequent resignation of President Richard Nixon — voted in Jimmy Carter, an outsider, to Washington. In 2016, a large enough portion of the electorate was sufficiently dissatisfied at governmental performance that it elevated Donald J. Trump to the highest office in the land.

And in 2020, a sufficient majority of Americans, dissatisfied with this alternative, elected Joe Biden to this office.

Much of my time in congressional leadership was marked by bitter inter-party strife, as manifested in the partial government shutdowns of 1995 and 1996. This breakdown of process was repeated in 2011 during the Obama Administration, and again in the first half of

2019 during the tenure of President Trump. My arrival in Washington came at a time when there was widely socialized uncertainty about America's role in the world and broad-based concern that our best days were behind us. The same concerns and issues plague us now.

But I remain highly optimistic because of my unshakeable belief in the democratic process, which I consider to be the highest manifestation of human social evolution ever witnessed on this planet. By telling my story — explaining how the process works through the lens of my experience and these deeply held beliefs — it is my hope that I am not only recounting the past but also offering my vision of a roadmap for the future.

"History doesn't repeat itself, but it does rhyme," Mark Twain famously said. What follows is my history. You can judge for yourself after reading this book whether my fellow Missourian was correct.

CHAPTER 1

A "Show Me" Childhood

In the same manner that the roads of political life point toward writing down stories, we can perhaps fairly state that the stories follow the path of that political life. A life story — most efficiently conveyed in chronological order. And I'm here to tell mine.

I would encourage readers to view this narrative very much as a story because, as I learned in the very formative stages of my path into politics, there is no more important element of the process than effective communication. Further, I have come to believe that the best means of communicating a message is through storytelling. I first realized this at the inspiration of C. Oscar Johnson, the minister of the Third Baptist Church in St. Louis where my family worshipped during my childhood. Our minister was a wonderful storyteller, and therefore — at least to me — an outstanding purveyor of the Message of God.

Let's begin at the beginning, shall we? I was born on January 31, 1941 — less than a year before the United States entered the Second World War — to Louis Andrew and Loreen Cassell Gephardt in St. Louis, the metropolitan center of Missouri: the "Show Me" State. The phrase "Show Me" became Missouri's motto through the words of one of my predecessors, Democratic Congressman Willard Duncan Vandiver. During an 1899 speech in Philadelphia, he said:

"I come from a state that raises corn and cotton and cockleburs and Democrats, and frothy eloquence neither convinces nor satisfies me. I am from Missouri. You have got to show me." And he was right. The Missouri that I grew up in and still know today is a place that believes in action, not rhetoric.

My background and early experiences should serve to illustrate the point. At the time of my birth, my father was a driver for Pevely Dairy where he worked for three decades. He was a milkman. In other words, he would wake up every morning at 4 a.m., load up his vehicle (a process that involved breaking through ice in the freezers where the milk was stored), and deliver dairy products to all the customers on his South St. Louis route — most of whom he got to know personally. I had the experience of accompanying him many times on his morning deliveries. The memories of his dedication, hard work, and good spirit have remained with me always.

My father grew up on a farm, one of a family of seven children, and I have no doubt that his upbringing contributed greatly to his worth ethic and other personality traits. Bear in mind that he was a child of the Great Depression. He came of age in an era where the responsibility of providing shelter, clothing, and food for one's own was often a daily struggle. It's one that I knew my parents felt very deeply. Among other ways that he demonstrated this was through a deep aversion to debt of any kind. Though we never discussed it much, he no doubt bore witness to many farmers in his community who found themselves, through no fault of their own but rather as the result of broad-based economic collapse, unable to repay the loans they had taken out to run their businesses. It is perhaps for this reason that not only did my dad never borrow a dime for discretionary purposes, but he was also borderline obsessive in paying bills the moment he received them. Even now, I can still see him returning from the mailbox every day — writing out the checks to pay for any bills — and then just as immediately, going out to post them.

Dad was also a proud Teamster of thirty years standing. He believed in the union and in the concept of unions in general. He often told me that it was only the presence of the union that enabled guys like him to get a fair shake. I never forgot these sentiments; in fact, they informed much of my political career.

Other than that, Lou was a quiet man and a good husband and father. He seldom had a great deal to say, but he was always there taking us on camping trips and supporting us in our path to adulthood. My dad often chaperoned Cub and Boy Scout camping trips. Eventually, I became an Eagle Scout — I think there's an obvious connection here.

Dad and I were big fans of the St. Louis Cardinals baseball team. My childhood came before television was widely available, but we listened to every contest on radio station KMOX, which broadcasts the games to this day. As a young boy, we'd attend games at the old Sportsman's Park. It was a golden age for the team. Branch Rickey, a marginal player for the team, became an outstanding manager and developer of talent. And, while he left the Cardinals to join the Brooklyn Dodgers in 1942, his farm system produced such future stars as Enos Slaughter, Red Schoendienst and my hero: Stan Musial. Driven by "Stan the Man," the Cardinals won three World Series Championships in the 1940s.

But out in Brooklyn, Mr. Rickey was building a powerhouse that would come back to haunt the Cards. In 1947, as his most memorable achievement, he promoted Jackie Robinson to the majors and broke baseball's longstanding color line. It is hard looking back at that bold move from the standpoint of the present and appreciate the full significance of this event. Robinson, an all-time great, was the victim of racism — often devolving into violence — across all his baseball career. But, of course, he rose above this cycle of hate to become the universally revered figure he still is today. In 1997, forty years after his last plate appearance, Major League Baseball retired his number "42" across the sport, the first ever such honor awarded to any other player in any form of competition. (In 2000, the National Hockey League followed this example and permanently retired Wayne Gretzky's 99 across the league).

As a young boy, I bore direct witness to what Jackie had endured. We would occasionally attend games, and even back then, I couldn't fail to notice that almost the entire crowd was all white. Then Jackie came to town, slashing doubles, stealing bases, stealing home, and African Americans in St. Louis began coming out to show their support. They cheered for Robinson's heroics which infuriated the white Cardinals fans. Fights started breaking out between Black and White fans. I remember my dad quickly ushering me out of the stadium after a Dodger visit to make sure nothing untoward happened.

Of course, all of this foreshadowed the Civil Rights Movement that began to take shape in earnest about a decade later. However, as a boy I can remember human impacts of segregation and racial discrimination. In the St. Louis of the forties and fifties, schools, movie theaters — virtually all forms of entertainment — were race-specific, as were churches and even drinking fountains. While we still have a significant road to travel, I am pleased to have born witness, and to a certain extent participated in, the dawn and the evolution of the critical advancement of human rights embodied in the Civil Rights Movement.

My mother was the more outgoing of my parents. She was born in De Soto, MO, a small town about fifty miles southwest of St. Louis, the daughter of a train conductor for the Pullman line. She was an energetic and active young woman, playing basketball and tennis during high school. She taught me how to use a racquet and encouraged me to exercise every day of my life. Mom used to say to me: "Dick — use it or lose it!" She lived to be ninety-five, and, up to six months before her death, her morning routine featured sit ups, pushups, and other forms of working out.

I've tried the best I can to follow her example in this regard, but it's not easy.

Loreen was a religious woman and supervised the family's attendance at the above-mentioned third Baptist Church: twice every Sunday and once on Wednesday nights. Her guiding principle was the Golden Rule: "Do unto others as you would have them do unto you." But she had her own special way of expressing this. "Dick" she would always tell me, "You're gonna get back what you give out." She made the golden rule very understandable to me. She told me "Before you say anything to anybody — think how you would like it said to you. Before you do anything to anybody — think how you would like it done to you". I many times failed to heed her teaching — but her vivid explanation of this was by far the most important guiding principle of my life.

When I was very young, she was a stay-at-home mom. But after the Second World War, to help the family make ends meet, she entered the workforce, first as a legal secretary and then as the administrative manager of a local oxygen company. Her work ethic was also a great inspiration to me, and she always encouraged me to give all I had to every job I ever held. "If you don't have anything to do, find something useful to do for the company," was her advice to me.

My brother Don, who passed away a few years ago, was the musician of the family. While my friends and I were outside playing sports or war games (in the aftermath of the Second World War, most of the boys around me were fascinated by war and would dress up as soldiers and engage in mock battles), Don could always be found practicing scales on his clarinet or saxophone. He went on to be a professor of music and humanities, and eventually Dean of Fine and Performing Arts at Rowan University in Glassboro, NJ.

My family was not particularly political. My parents took care to vote in every election and were informed as to public affairs (on both a local and national level), but were not actively involved in the political process. Being from The Greatest Generation, and having endured through the Great Depression, the Second World War, and the Korean War, they felt that their calling was home and family. As should be apparent from the story thus far, while we lacked for nothing growing up, money was always scarce. We experienced the impact of product shortages from their coming of age until I was a teenager. Until several years beyond the end of the Second World War, the country was under rationing, with each family receiving weekly coupons for the purchase of a fixed supply of meat. Virtually nobody in our acquaintance could afford discretionary luxury items. Nylon stockings, for instance, was an indulgence about which women could only dream. Most families had no cars or used cars and spent many spare hours maintaining them and repairing them.

Thus, I remember vividly, the year 1955 when I was in my mid-high school period, a neighbor came home with a brand spanking new '55 Chevrolet Bel Air — two-toned, charcoal black and chartreuse. Everyone in the neighborhood came out to admire this miracle of transportation lavishness. I can't exactly explain why, but this event in my mind signaled in a new and more prosperous age. There was a Ford dealer across the street from my high school, and many of us showed up at the dealer to see the new Ford models on the day in the fall when they were revealed. The 1955 Ford Fairlane with a chrome stripe across the roof was met with surprise and delight.

Moving on to my education, I attended Mason Elementary School in South St. Louis, where all of the teachers were unmarried women — like nuns, but without having taken the vows. Given the circumstances and the age, I must say that the curriculum was surprisingly rigorous. Our teachers made sure we left there with a full grounding in the three Rs, and a strong sense of how to interact within our community.

I continued my education in the public school system, attending Southwest High School in St. Louis. It was here that the future course of my life began to take shape. I began to show an interest in communication arts, involving myself in activities such as drama, public speaking, and debate. One teacher in particular took notice. Ms. Meenach, a single lady and dedicated educator, believed that I showed some promise and encouraged me to apply for a scholarship sponsored by the National High School Institute for a summer program at Northwestern University. She told me that if my parents approved, she would help me complete the forms and submit the application. Well, she did, and I was accepted.

Thus, in the summer of 1957, having never travelled outside of the St. Louis metropolitan area, I boarded a train to Chicago and then Evanston, IL, to spend five weeks with some of the best and brightest young people from across the country who had gathered on the Lake Michigan campus of Northwestern University. We interacted through disciplines such as drama and debate, and I am proud to tell you that I was even selected for the role of Professor Henry Higgins in a version of Pygmalion that was part of the program!

Thankfully, though, that was pretty much the beginning and the end of my acting career. The soaring talent of the many fine performers attending the conference convinced me that this was not my arena.

And, of course, the fates had other plans for me.

But I will always remember and remain grateful to Ms. Meenach for seeing something in me, believing in me, and encouraging me to extend my reach to points beyond my grasp. I have often thought of what my future would have been if she had not helped me at a turning point in my life.

Later that same summer, I was also fortunate enough to win a scholarship to attend a two-week camp session sponsored by the American Youth Foundation. Camp Miniwanca, the brainchild of Ralston Purina Corporation Founder William H. Danforth, was a Michigan-based enterprise devoted to the development of the leadership skills of young people from diverse backgrounds. It still exists, in fact thrives, to this day. Here I had the opportunity to gain further access to the wonders of higher education as many college professors held seminars for the campers.

These experiences shaped my future, and upon graduating from high school in 1959, helped form my determination to attend college. For many of the present generation, this may seem like a logical, intuitive step to take for a recent high school graduate, but for me, it was rather profound. Neither of my parents even graduated from high school, and no one thought about a path to college for me.

But I was determined, and after my summer experience the only university that I even considered was Northwestern. So, I applied, was accepted, obtained a scholarship, and enrolled.

My experience as an undergraduate at Northwestern was everything that I hoped it would be and more. I enrolled as a drama and speech student, but after a year transferred to a major that carried the moniker Public Address and Group Communication. Under today's university protocols, it is more simply deemed Communications Studies. This is a major that I would enthusiastically recommend to anyone considering entering the field of public service or to anyone else — period! As I suggested above, effective communication is at the core of the human experience, and success in any endeavor seems to be highly correlated with the effectiveness of the communications process. Whether you enter a field like Finance, Medicine, or Law, or whether it's simply a matter of establishing the best possible relations with loved ones, the better you are able to share thoughts and ideas, the better off you'll be.

The curriculum for a communications degree was rich and diverse. I took courses in Language, Linguistic Inadequacies, Thought, and Semantics. Several classes involved the formation of groups for theoretical problem solving and an evaluation of how to best operate in such a context. This, of course, was invaluable training for my future career in government.

In summary, it was a spectacular college experience.

During my undergraduate years, I took a formal interest in politics. Looking back, I can't say specifically what forces drove me in that direction, other than the fact that my course load involved teaching me how to give speeches. I thought politics was a reasonable means of both further honing these skills and putting them to best use. Clearly, though, I had an interest in the political process. This interest grew over time. I added a minor in Political Science and History and studied these disciplines assiduously.

I thought about running for office in high school but never did. But at Northwestern, I ran for Vice President of my sophomore class and won. Two years later, I was elected Student Body President. I remember with gratitude all of the encouragement and support I received from fellow classmates during this period. I believe that their inspiration carried me well-beyond the winning of college elections, into my successes in the broader political arena.

I want to emphasize that this is the point that the concept I referenced at the beginning of this chapter — the use of stories to communicate — really took hold for me. I found back then, and through the course of my subsequent career, that the conveyance of information through general language often failed to fully capture a listener's attention and focus. Tell them a story, though, and you've got them.

Some of my most important anecdotes come from my remembrances of stories told to me by the minister from the third Baptist Church in St. Louis, which I attended all throughout my childhood.

One that resonated with me throughout my life (and which I have retold many times) is based upon his recollection of a teenage boy from a small town in rural Missouri. His parents always told him about an elderly neighbor who was the most respected person in the village, due to his wide knowledge set. He could answer any question put to him by anyone.

One day, the young man decided to put forward a question intended to stump him, and, by doing so, supplant him as the wisest person in the town. First, he captured a small bird (alive), took it to the man's house and said: "Wise man, I have a bird behind my back. Is it alive or dead?" If the wise man answered "alive," he would choke the bird and show that he was dead. If the answer was "dead," he would open his hand and show him that the creature was still living.

He carried out his plan, and when he asked the wise man if the bird was alive or dead, the wise man, after a pause replied as follows:

"My son, that is up to you".

This little tale never failed to resonate with the listener, and it reinforced for me the power of storytelling — as opposed to direct language — as a means of conveying important messages.

At this point, I had no plan to enter public life, but the political bug was growing inside of me. At the encouragement of a few confidantes, I began to think about law school as my next step. In retrospect, this seems entirely sensible because if you planned to become either a lawmaker or an executor of the law, legal training would come in enormously handy. No doubt this is the reason that so many leading politicians are either lawyers, or at minimum, have legal training.

One of my closest undergraduate friends — my roommate, in fact — was a fellow named John McCollough. His father was a Democrat and the duly elected sheriff of a county in Northeast Oklahoma, which informed his interest in politics. He was full of stories of politicians from the state. John and I hatched a plan to apply to the University of Michigan Law School. Both of us were accepted, and, upon graduating from Northwestern in 1962, off to Ann Arbor we went.

We remained friends and roommates throughout.

I'll only cover one aspect of my law school experience. During my first semester, and in the midst of a grueling torts class, came the news that President Kennedy had been shot and killed in Dallas. The professor cut the lecture short, and we all went into the dean's office to watch the horrifying events unfold on a small black and white television in his office. For me and many of my peers, the Kennedy assassination was a signal event in our lives. We all had great admiration and took great inspiration from John F. Kennedy. He was our role model, the one many of us aspired to emulate, if only with partial success. For me, he was the greatest communicator of them all: smart, cogent, assertive, self-effacing, funny, and he almost never failed to convey his message effectively, with style, and in his own way. Even today, listening to his old speeches — the Berlin speech, his Inaugural Address, and so many others — the fire still burns.

We were all further inspired that someone like him, with such a multitude of gifts — looks, intelligence, charm, wealth, access — would devote his life to public service. If he could do it, perhaps in ways large and small, so could we, or at least this is what we thought. And then, in the flash of an instant, it was all over. But again, his light never burned out, his fire never extinguished itself, and we carried on.

And I will close this chapter with one final thought. The Kennedy Assassination can be viewed as the exception that proves the rule, or shall we say the theme of this memoir: politics as a substitute for violence. On that horrible November day in 1963, these two worlds collided, and we were all the worse for it. Back then and carrying forward into the future, we must draw such lessons and take such actions to guard — with all our might — against recurrence.

CHAPTER 2

A Door-to-Door Journey to the Halls of Congress

My political interest grew across my years at University of Michigan Law School. Of course, I discussed this with many people whose opinion I valued, and through these discussions, two potential paths emerged. Most of those to whom I reached out encouraged me to go to Washington immediately, ideally as a Congressional staff member. In this way, so they told me, I would become exposed to political life and thus have the ability make an informed decision as to whether I really wanted to dedicate my career to politics.

But as the poet Robert Frost once famously wrote, "I took the road less traveled." I easily decided that because getting elected in politics required convincing people to vote for you, it made more sense to me to go back home and engage in grassroots politics at the lowest level.

I've always believed that to master any profession or activity, it's best to start at the lowest rung on the ladder. Only in this manner can one learn how things are done and how to conduct yourself. So I went back to St. Louis to my home turf of the 14th Ward — an area known as South St. Louis. In 1966 I married Jane Gephardt, who I met at Northwestern and who grew up in Columbus, Nebraska. We started a family and I accepted an offer to become an associate at one of the City's largest law firms, Thompson Mitchell.

At that time, the Vietnam War was under way, with U.S. involvement expanding. I was of draft age, and, at the suggestion of some friends, I enlisted in the Air National Guard. I was soon off to basic training at Lackland Air Force Base in San Antonio, Texas. The program lasted about five or six weeks, after which I was dispatched to a unit in St. Louis which featured F-4 jet fighter planes that were in heavy use by our military in Southeast Asia. We were advised of the strong likelihood that we would be called to the front lines, and I did my best to prepare for that harrowing experience.

However, as it happened, my legal training and law degree rendered me eligible to apply to become Legal Officer for the unit as a vacancy had recently opened. This required more training (this time with the Joint Army Group), which I undertook at Scott Air Force Base in St. Clair County, IL — right across the river from the St. Louis metro area.

I emerged from that training having won that post at the rank of First Lieutenant. Eventually, I rose to the rank of Captain of the Air Force.

Among my other duties, I supervised the Mobility Unit. This process mostly involved overseeing monthly drills under which all personnel were required to report to the base within twenty-four hours, in full gear, at unannounced points around the calendar year. Once there, we loaded the crew onto military jets in full simulation of a bona fide dispatch to the front lines. It was a lot of work, but I really enjoyed the people and some of the men in the unit became my lifelong friends.

I did three two-year stints in the Air National Guard, but I never made it to Vietnam.

Through it all, my main ambitions continued to reside in the political arena. I began asking around as to how I could involve myself and found out that the best place to get started was at the ward or precinct level.

Of course, there was a Democratic Party organization attached to the 14th Ward; so I decided to pay them a visit.

At the time I took this step, I knew no one who knew anything about local politics. So, when I wandered into a ward meeting at an American Legion Hall, I had no idea what to expect. There, I encountered a smoke-filled room that very closely resembled the caricatures of a political organization. Most of the precinct workers were, in one form or another, employed in city government — typically in the circuit court offices, but also in such divisions as the Parks Department.

The atmosphere brought to mind images of the Chicago Political Machine; but it was 1965, and this is the manner in which political organizations operated at the time. I can't say it was overly elegant or sophisticated, but I judge that it served its purpose for the time and place. I'm sure that upon first impression at that meeting I stuck out like a sore thumb: a young recent law school grad entering the lair of grizzled ward workers and other political veterans. I got the sense that these political operatives had been coming to ward meetings since time immemorial.

Most likely, they had to as a condition of keeping their jobs.

I stuck around, and by doing so I was introduced to the first of many influences on my real-life path into politics; Mr. Phelim O'Toole, the clerk of the Circuit Court of St. Louis. At the time of our introduction, he was already in his seventies or perhaps his eighties. He suffered from acute arthritis that left him a wheelchair bound. I can still remember him being wheeled around with a big cigar in his mouth. He was a very nice man, but when he met me his first reaction was one of wonder as to who I was and what in the world I was doing there. I told him I wanted to engage in politics, specifically by volunteering to be part of Democratic Ward Organization.

He kind of looked at me like I was crazy and then he said, "Well, if you want to do something you can take the second precinct. I'll make you the precinct captain of the Second Precinct." I said, "Great, what do I have to do?" At which point he informed me that my job was to go door-to-door and meet everybody in the precinct. He even offered me a map.

"Introduce yourself and try to find out — if you can without being objectionable — if the folks tend to be more Democratic or more Republican in their voting behavior," he instructed me. "Keep a list and mark down for each name whether you think they're a Democrat or a Republican. And then the next part of your job is that on Election Day we have a sample ballot that we hand out with all the Democratic candidates named on it. And I want you to stand at the polling place and hand out the ballot. You need to be there at 6:00 in the morning.

You can't go to work that day," he concluded. Bear in mind that I had recently accepted a position at a large local law firm. They were well aware of my interest in politics when I took the job (I had informed them), and, while they probably didn't understand my thinking, they very graciously accommodated me. When Election Day rolled around, Mr. O'Toole instructed me to check my list of Democratic voters and identify any who had not showed up at the polls by 4 p.m. I was then to leave the polling place, get in my car, and round up the stragglers. I had a few hours to do so, because the polls didn't close until 7 or 8 p.m.

In today's political nomenclature this process is called Ballot Harvesting, and it has been the subject of considerable controversy recently. I won't offer an explicit judgment about the system, but will state that it has existed in one form or another for many centuries — and is likely to endure. Bringing in the vote is what grassroots politics has always been about, what it's about today, and, in my judgment, what it will be about in the future. As a politician or political operative, your objective is to get voters to the polls, and, of course, to persuade them to vote for the candidates for whom you are advocating.

One way or another, this was the beginning of my door-to-door approach to politics.

So, I continued. I attended all the ward meetings, and through this process I had the privilege of meeting high-quality candidates at the local, state, and national level. My first experience with a big-time national political figure occurred during a city-wide Democratic Party Dinner amid the 1968 Presidential Election. Hubert Humprhey, the Democratic candidate for Vice President, was the featured guest. Through these events and others, my conviction that I had chosen the right path for myself continued to grow.

Approximately one year into my tenure as Precinct Captain, Mr. O'Toole passed away. It devolved to a committee woman named Margaret Butler to appoint his successor. She had noticed my commitment and work product and asked me if I wanted to succeed him.

Naturally, I was thrilled to accept that appointment! But I informed her at the time that my real ambition was to run for political office, most likely as an Alderman. She had no problem with this and suggested that, because the next aldermanic election was a couple of years away, running the ward meetings would be great training for the election and the elected position itself.

I learned a great deal from Ms. Butler. She taught me not only how the City Council operated, but she paved the way for my fluid interaction with committee members and aldermen from other wards. Also, she opened my eyes as to the power of advertising in the political process (a subject to which we will return later in the chapter).

With the approach of Spring in 1971, and with the full blessing of Ms. Butler, I made the decision to run for alderman in the 14th Ward. Her advice was simply to continue the approach I had taken as Precinct Captain — only on a broader scale. I needed, again, to knock on every door in the ward, ideally armed with campaign literature. In addition, she strongly encouraged me to place as many yard signs as possible on the lawns of my would-be constituents. "Name recognition," she advised me, "will be the key to your success."

The incumbent that I sought to unseat was a Republican named Ray Summers — a very nice guy, but not the most dynamic of political forces or likely to set the City Hall afire.

I began my efforts in earnest shortly after New Year's Day, 1971. The air was cold and there was snow on the ground. And beyond whatever physical discomfort I was feeling as I went door-to-door, I was worried that the voters would think that I looked too young to be an alderman. I'm not sure how effective this was, but to protect against the elements and to project a more mature persona, I always wore a hat on these sojourns.

Knocking on the doors of untold numbers of strangers was a rather surreal exercise, but I did it. I introduced myself, spoke about my platform, asked them if they had any questions, and left them with the literature I prepared (more about this later). It was really a wonderful experience because I learned a lot about the voters in my district. I discovered what they cared about and what they were interested in. I heard their stories, where they came from, how long they had lived in the neighborhood, and what issues concerned them most. Though hardly surprising in retrospect, many of their concerns were those of a very personal nature: unrepaired potholes, poorly paved streets, trees that needed trimming, and even the corpses of dead dogs left in alleyways.

I was particularly struck by the depth of their anxieties concerning the decay of neighborhoods. Bear in mind that it was 1971, and residents were justifiably worried about urban blight, declining population (including, admittedly, the specter of "white flight"), and attendant disincentive for homeowners to invest in the maintenance and upkeep of their properties. All of this catalyzed a commitment to the refurbishment of neighborhoods on the decline and to make it a focus of my campaign.

The primary was scheduled for March, but I was running unopposed in the Democratic Party, so there was no problem there. I was able to focus my attention directly on the general election, which was to take place in April. As mentioned above, I had prepared some homespun literature that I pecked out on a manual typewriter and then copied on an old-fashioned, hand crank mimeograph machine. My total expenditure for the campaign was on the order of one hundred dollars.

And then came election night itself. At that time, vote tallies were conveyed by precinct captains who would physically count the ballots in their precincts and report the totals back to ward headquarters, a storefront on Kingshighway in South St. Louis.

When all the precincts save one had come in, I was about three or four votes behind. The final result came down to the outcome in a precinct run by a gentleman named Fred Kaufman, who was also a clerk in one of the circuit courts in downtown. I can still remember his election night entrance, with his big, gruff figure walking toward me and a grim look on his face. At that point, I was sure we had lost the election. But then a huge smile emerged, and he greeted me with a hug.

We had won by twelve votes.

I can only view this as one of a handful of inflection points in my political career. I'm pretty sure if I had lost that election, I would not have run again for anything else. But there I was, Alderman for the 14th Ward, in the City of St. Louis.

I remember the excitement of going to my first meeting of the Board of Alderman and meeting my new colleagues, half of whom were African Americans. The split was pretty much across the geographic lines of the city, with the majority of representatives from the north being Black, and the other half — including my jurisdiction in South St. Louis — being white. The neighborhoods were experiencing racial, cultural, and demographic changes, but that was the lay of the land when I took office.

In 1971, the Dean of the Board of Aldermen was an older gentleman named Red Villa, a legend in that legislative body. He owned a bar on the banks of the Mississippi in South St. Louis, right near a factory where they made barges for use on the river. He was a big man with a big personality, very gregarious, and famous for greeting customers from early in the morning until late at night. And he took me under his wing.

Red was like Tip O'Neill, the Speaker of the House when I got to Congress. One day, early in my tenure, he said: "Young man if you want to get re-elected you've got to remember one thing: the people that voted for you care more about the hole in the street which they dropped their wheel into every day and night, the tree that's not been trimmed, the sidewalk that they're tripping over that's uneven and wrong, and the dead dog in the alley, than they do about the city budget or any other big city-wide issue that you're going to be dealing with here.

"And if you take care with real hard work of those problems that people will bring to you — day and night — then you will have a great chance to be re-elected." This brought to my mind the famous Tip

O'Neill quote that all politics is local. It was a great lesson, a reminder that while St. Louis was a big city with big city issues, and no shortage of sizeable challenges to tackle, but it is imperative to remember that you are a public servant, and you have to take care of the people that you represent in your jurisdiction.

Retaining their trust is a matter of "customer service." The electorate is the customer, and if you don't serve it properly, then you won't get re-elected. It's as simple as that.

Red gave me another insight that I've never forgotten. The job of government is to extract monies from the citizenry — in the form of taxes — and spend it in a very judicious way that allows people to see the benefit of these levies.

Of course, no one likes paying taxes. But my experience is that most people accept this obligation, provided that the government can demonstrate that taxpayers are getting value for these outlays. The public is entitled to a return on the hard-earned money they must turn over to enable governments to function. And one can see that if everybody in government abided by this principle, it really does make a great deal of sense. However, like much else in life, what is logical and intuitive in principle is often very difficult to achieve in terms of action.

But just as I was embarking on my aldermanic journey, a momentous event happened in my personal life. In May 1972, my son Matt was diagnosed with terminal cancer at St. Louis Children's Hospital. They had found an aggressive tumor on his prostrate, which was invading his entire abdomen.

The attending physician estimated that he had six weeks to live.

My wife Jane and I were, quite naturally, devastated. We prayed day and night for his recovery.

Soon, a young, resilient doctor named Abdel Ragab, who had researched Matt's tumor, excitedly informed us of a triple drug chemotherapy treatment, which, applied in conjunction with aggressive radiation, might shrink the tumor sufficiently so that it could be surgically removed.

He told us that it was a long shot, and that the side effects of radiation could cause more damage. He left it up to us as to whether to proceed with the treatment regimen. God certainly blessed Matt, his family and us. He is our gift from God and modern medicine.

We decided it was worth the risk, and, after this treatment cycle, along with six or seven subsequent surgeries to overcome the side effects of radiation, he survived. In 2020, he, along with his wife Tricia and their two wonderful children, celebrated his fiftieth birthday.

I include this highly personal anecdote to reinforce the notion that politicians and elected officials face the same real-world problems as everyone else. Meanwhile, the wheels of government continue to spin, forcing everyone to re-examine their priorities and adjust.

So it goes in government, so it goes in life.

I was one of five first-term aldermen that the local press began to refer to as the Young Turks, mostly because we worked together as a group with a common set of objectives. At the top of our list was improvement of the streets and sidewalks in the wards we represented, many of which were in a shameful state of incompletion and disrepair. In some cases, sidewalks existed but without curbs. In other areas, the streets were unpaved except for a kind of gravel.

All of this created a disincentive for residents to invest in their own dwellings. After all, if you live on a broken street without proper sidewalks, why maintain or upgrade your house?

Public infrastructure improvement was our top priority, and in order to achieve our objectives, we had to deal with the full Board of Aldermen and the City's Mayor, a vibrant, salesman-like gentleman named Alfonso J. Cervantes. Al was also a developer in St. Louis who made a lot of money building hotels and other commercial structures. At the point of the arrival of the Young Turks, he was promoting a three percent sales tax increase, mostly for the General Purpose Fund. He needed our votes to pass the bill, and we agreed, on the condition that one-third of the new revenues would be allocated for the improvement of city streets and sidewalks. This was a big ask because St. Louis had many needs (fire department, police, schools, etc.) and a declining tax base. As such, it was under a constant burden of fiscal duress. Al would certainly have preferred to reject our demands, but he needed our votes, so the agreement came to fruition.

And then the project work that we envisioned began and continued through in my first term on the Board of Aldermen. By the time I was nearing the end of my aldermanic career, we had made a great deal of progress, which residents could see before their very eyes.

I believe that this gave us significant political capital because it was visible throughout the city.

The streets were cleaner and functioned better, neighborhood trees came alive, and those dead dogs disappeared. But the biggest, most gratifying improvements of all were the upgrades of the properties themselves. Seeing neighborhood renovations led to a Pavlovian response under which property owners began to clean up their lawns, paint their houses, and even build that spare bedroom addition, which previously — after years of urban decay — made no sense from an investment perspective. Now, suddenly, property upgrades were a logical investment, and there was a natural, pride-based incentive to maintain and upgrade your home.

In the end, the essential element of democracy is its unique ability to get people with diverse ethnicities, backgrounds and beliefs to work together to support one another. It is based on an understanding that, like it or not, we are all tied together. If a child does not get educated it hurts all of us. If someone is unhealthy — it affects all of us. Democracy has allowed our urban centers to not only survive but grow and provide a good life for millions upon millions of Americans. It allows us to "work together " which is the way humans came to dominate the earth. When we were hunter gathers in groups of 80 or 100 — group members collaborated, cooperated and worked together to survive. Now cities are millions of people and America is 340 million people and the most successful nation on earth BECAUSE we are a democracy where we work together for the common good. It is not an overstatement to conclude that democracy is the highest expression of human evolution.

Note that my focus extended beyond my own 14th Ward. I was involved in urban renewal on a city-wide basis. Given my legal training and my status as a lawyer in good standing at the Missouri Bar, I was in an ideal position to assist with such processes as filling out and filing various applications and reports. I even helped set up neighborhood corporations —work that I always performed on a pro bono basis.

The last of these initiatives catalyzed our planning of neighborhood festivals all across the city. In addition to the benefits attendant to neighborhood, social, and ethnic pride, we were also able to use these forums as fund-raising mechanisms for various civic-minded initiatives.

Moreover, the festivals provided an efficient framework for public advocacy and the socialization of the political issues that were most important to the Young Turks, to the city, and to me personally.

Beyond urban renewal, our top issue was the education system. The St. Louis school programs were in decline at the time and vastly in need of upgrades. The only means of funding this was through the real estate tax system. As indicated above, tax increases were and are always controversial and difficult to pass. But I was and am a huge believer in the public education system, of which I am a product, and through which I was able to achieve everything that I accomplished in this life. Here I always reflect back on the great teachers that mentored me.

So I worked hard on education reform and finance. I set my focus on improving the City's education system and am proud to say that every associated funding initiative I worked on passed eventually.

My last major memory of my experience on the St. Louis Board of Aldermen takes us back to the concept of urban renewal. As I witnessed the structural upgrades across the city, I noticed that the removal of large trash items was an increasingly intractable problem. Yes, the roads were improved, the houses were repainted, etc., but invariably, that old refrigerator or washer dryer lay rusting on the street. The city simply did not have the resources to provide this removal service. So one day I called the Department of Sanitation and asked if I could borrow a garbage truck. They allowed me to do so.

Every Saturday in 1975, I led a group of volunteers (including my dad) and we traveled through the alleys of my ward to pick up big trash items. Let me tell you, we picked up a lot of large, unsightly garbage, and I often wonder decades later how my back survived the experience.

From my perspective, this only added to and reinforced the palpable sense of pride that residents felt about their civic surroundings. And pride led to action. The ranks of volunteers swelled, and homeowners began investing in their houses and their communities. I believe that my political approach worked, and, in 1975, I ran for re-election and won with a much wider margin than I had enjoyed the first time around.

On the whole, in terms of politics at the metro level, while much has changed, much remains the same since my time as a councilman. All of the good and bad of political frameworks are on display at this level. But perhaps more of its underbelly is visible due to the finite nature of an urban constituency. Now, as then, there's give and take; deals are negotiated, and it is impossible for any political agent to fully realize his or her agenda. However, as I suggested in the Introduction (and as will be a theme throughout this book), there is a beauty in the humanity of the process. Virtually everyone agrees that cities must be governed, and that such government must be administered by mere mortals — flawed-human-beings, rendering the process all-the-more poignant. There is reward and gratification not only in the successes achieved, but even in the case of failure, which, if accepted with proper spirit, can offer an opportunity to learn.

Shortly after my re-election, the city turned its political attention to the upcoming Mayoral election. As an ambitious Young Turk, I strongly considered throwing my hat in the ring. However, just as I was contemplating this bold move came the announcement that Lenore Sullivan, my district's generation-long representative to the United States Congress, would not seek another term.

So I shifted my objectives from the mayor's office to the halls of Congress; and this time it didn't require much thought. The very day after Congresswoman Sullivan's announcement, I went to Jefferson City, Missouri, and filed on the spot to run for the U.S. House of Representatives. Around this same time, Don Gralick, a State Senator and the Head of the St. Louis Electrical Workers Union (a very prominent Democrat in the city), filed to run against me in the primary. Joe Badaracco, President of the Board of Alderman, filed on the Republican side.

Everyone with whom I spoke said that given the credentials and the profile of my two opponents I really had no chance of winning. But they encouraged me to press on, nonetheless, for the benefit of the experience — which serves so often as the consolation prize for falling short of victory itself.

But I wasn't in it for the experience — I wanted to win. The challenge was to figure out how to take on these formidable opponents. I decided that I had to keep doing what I'd always done since I entered politics a decade earlier: going door to door. But the process of ringing doorbells in an election for a city ward with around 10,000 constituents is much different from that which applies to a Congressional District with a population fifty times as large (500,000).

The only way to proceed was to commit myself — day and night — to the effort. Recall that at the time I still held my law firm day job, and the attention needed to perform effectively in this position was clearly incompatible with my campaign strategy. I met with my bosses and offered to take an unpaid sabbatical. However, they were gracious enough to support my efforts and even kept me on the payroll throughout the campaign.

Every day and every night throughout much of 1976, I went out to meet my would-be constituents with my wife and parents in tow. By my estimate, we visited approximately 50,000 homes. Along the way, I noticed that Labor Leader Gralick had yard signs in front of many of the homes I visited. This chilled me — I remembered well what Ms. Butler had told me about the importance of these displays and knew that I couldn't compete with the sheer numbers of his signage campaign. Therefore, I decided that the only way to respond was to put up signs of my own, but to locate them on major streets and arteries within the district to achieve maximum visibility with minimum resources. Without that, no one would have known who I was.

I spent about a month going up and down the main intersections within the district and putting up homemade yard signs that my father and a few friends helped me construct. But this was not my only issue: I needed also to devise a plan for the expensive process of TV advertising. In the Missouri of 1976, televised political ad campaigns were not as ubiquitous as they are at present, but they were important, nonetheless. I hadn't spent much money on yard signs and decided to reserve what funds that I had raised (mostly from friends, family, and my own limited store of capital) for a TV advertising campaign timed close to the election itself.

We put all our money into TV in advance of the August primary contest. And somehow we won with a visible majority. It was a miraculous result given the point from which we started.

By my recollection, between the primary and the general election, we spent the tidy sum of $70,000 — all from family and friends and my own limited resources. And we won the primary — a huge deal!

The 1976 Presidential Election was a contest between Jimmy Carter and Gerald Ford. Nixon had resigned in the summer of 1974, and by September, President Ford had pardoned him. All of this cast a huge Watergate pall over the election. Naturally, this worked in my favor as a candidate on the Democratic side. Just as I had done in the primary, I continued to go door to door in my district. And the combination was a winner. I prevailed in the General Election by a similar margin by which I won the Democratic Primary.

At the ripe old age of thirty-five, I was on my way to Congress.

I took the Oath of Office in January of 1977, and my early days in the House were a real eye opener for me. In contrast to a local political landscape, at the national level, there was a much greater measure of diversity. Many of the members of Congress I met in the beginning had been serving their districts for ages. In 1976, the vast majority of seats in the South were held by Democrats — a reflection of the fact that the Democratic Party was the dominant party of the Confederate States.

Though it may sound strange, I do indeed believe that historical events have a long tail. And the Civil War was as important an event as perhaps any in American history. From my vantage-point, the associated impacts ring forward even into the present and will likely continue to do so well into the future.

Of course, many of these Southern Congressmen were older White males of long standing in the House. The Congress of the present day has a very different look, feel, and composition. And as I entered into my new responsibilities, it soon became clear that a key tactical objective was to secure appropriate committee membership assignments. In this effort I had a great mentor, Richard Bolling, the member from Kansas City. Even today, he is viewed as one of the greatest legislators in Congressional history.

Bolling was a Second World War veteran who had enlisted as a Private and risen to the rank of Lieutenant Colonel by the end of the conflict, having served in the war years as an assistant to the Chief of Staff of General Douglas MacArthur. He was also an educator who ultimately became a Professor at Boston College. At the time of my entrance on to the Congressional scene, he was running for the post of Majority Leader against two formidable opponents: Texas Congressman Jim Wright (who ultimately prevailed) and Phil Burton (a Democrat from California). But for many of the younger members of the House (over the 1974 and 1976 contests, approximately 120 new members of Congress were elected), Bolling was our man.

Congressman Bolling took an interest in me, and it didn't wane when he lost the race for Majority Leader. It was he who emphasized the importance of the right committee assignments as a path to success. At this time, it was highly unusual for a freshman congressman to be granted a post on the powerful House Ways and Means Committee (I may have been the first), but Bolling took up my cause and used whatever influence he could bring to bear on Speaker Tip O'Neill. Ultimately, I secured the assignment.

Serving on Ways and Means in my first year in Congress was a wonderful experience that I will never forget.

One truly plum assignment within Ways and Means is a place on the Budget Committee. And, within a couple of years, I was able to obtain a spot. This too was a great learning opportunity and a wonderful experience. Every day, the Budget Committee took up issues and voted upon matters of great impact on every part of American life. Tip O'Neill had just won the Speakership at that time, and he was adamant that the Congress he led perform at a very high level.

We held meetings every day of the week, as driven by O'Neil, who insisted that we work hard and generate the best product achievable for the American People. As mentioned above, his motto was that all politics were local, and he always encouraged his caucus to pay attention and take care of the home front. They were the ones who elected you and paid the taxes that fueled the engines of government. If you remembered this and acted accordingly, he told us, you would be re-elected, and deservingly so.

During orientation, one new member asked him what he thought was the most important thing to know about House membership and associated politics. His response was this: "never break your word. If you break your word you're finished. You will have no career. Nobody will ever trust you and nobody will believe you." This resonated with me.

About a year later, I was walking down the hall in the Capitol Building and I saw his unmistakable figure approaching me. He pulled me aside and said, "Kid, I need your vote on a bill." I don't even remember what the bill was about, but I wasn't prepared to offer any resistance to this great leader of mine, so I pledged my vote to him. I went home the next weekend to learn that voting for this particular bill would be political suicide for me. I came back to Washington on Monday scared out of my wits. Truly, I didn't know what to do. I couldn't justifiably vote for the bill, and I remembered what he said about never breaking my word.

He had always told us that if we ever had a problem, he would make himself available to us. So, I arranged for an appointment; he allotted me five minutes. As the meeting approached, I had no idea what I was going to say. He greeted me and asked, "What's the problem, kid?" I said,

"Mr. Speaker, I came to ask for my word back."

He gave me with a big smile and said that this was a really good response. He went on to say that I could have my word back. "If you'd come in here with some bullshit excuse about why you couldn't keep your word, you wouldn't have got your word back." And that was a lesson I never forgot, and one I was able to apply when I found myself in a position of House leadership. The organization runs on trust, and, if the senior members were to be placed in a position to accomplish anything, it was imperative that they know where individual members of their caucus stand on every issue.

All of this becomes even more important as the composition of society, and therefore, the House, changes over time. In my early days, it was indeed a diverse group, but nothing like the diversity that prevails today. In 1977 the Congress contained 21 women members. In 2023 Congress has 152 women members. In 1977 Congress contained 25 minority members. In 2023 Congress had 133 minority members.

But, as always, the wind blows both ways. In the 1960s, as the Democratic Party accelerated its migration to be the voice of the under-represented (as featured in such signal events as the passage of the Civil Rights and Voting Rights Acts in the mid-1960s), our party's hold on the South began to decline.

At present, the Democratic Party no longer holds a majority of seats in the South, and most of southern Democratic congressmen are

African American. Missouri is a border state, and at the beginning of my term, the majority of its representatives were White. One notable exception was Representative Bill Clay of St. Louis, Missouri, whose Congressional tenure began in the sixties, and who was one of the founders of the Black Congressional Caucus. He was a friend and advisor to me, and one whose kind assistance I'll never forget.

My story thus far in our narrative is one that is graced by the presence of outstanding mentors guiding my path throughout. My parents, my high school teachers, those I met through the scholarship programs — all of them lighted the way for me — and I like to think brought the best out of me.

I also must mention that my entire public service would not have been possible without the constant love and support of my wife, Jane, and my entire family — children, mother, father, brother Don and his family. Also, the thousands of staffers, employees, volunteers and VOTERS who supported my efforts to serve for over 40 years. You cannot deliver public service without the love and support of lots of your fellow citizens. This is one of the magic ingredients of self-government — "of, by and for" the PEOPLE. Over all those years I saw clearly how self-government actually works. In the end, the PEOPLE have to WANT to DO IT. And I have unending gratitude for all the people who allowed me the opportunity to do public service.

I cannot close this chapter without offering my admiration and appreciation to the competent, dedicated, and committed professionals in government that do most of the heavy lifting which supports the legislative process. They exist in all departments — Treasury, State, Health and Human Services, the Interior, Agriculture, etc. Some of them have spent their entire careers there. In current times, they are often criticized as being part of some embedded bureaucracy that controls government behind the scenes, while elected officials smile before cameras and make a show of legislating. But that was not my experience. These were proud, dedicated public servants to whom we all owed a considerable debt of gratitude.

Consider the Legislative Counsel's Office where experts painstakingly draft bills. Without them, the wheels of government would turn very slowly or perhaps not at all. I remember the first Carter Tax Bill, whose passage was principally the responsibility of the Ways and Means Committee. In those days, members from both parties worked together to draft legislation. In this particular instance, however, the White House wrote the original draft and presented it to Congress where it went to a bi-partisan process called a mark-up. This legislation was managed through the auspices of the Joint Tax Committee, which worked in support of taxation matters under Ways and Means. We worked for days and days on this particular bill, with every member from both parties seeking favored treatment for select constituents.

Through the exercise of writing a tax bill, it is easy to hand out breaks to special interests, and the process can take on a life of its own. In the case of this bill, things got out of hand — so much so that the Deputy Secretary of Treasury for Tax Policy, Larry Woodworth, called a special session and demanded that we end the handouts lest we consign the government and taxpayers to full-on insolvency. So, we came together to give it another go and to draft a realistic, affordable bill that would truly serve the interests of the American public. It was only through his leadership that we were able to succeed. It was a matter of credibility, experience, and trust.

There was a lot of give and take, and it was through this type of dynamic that the business of the nation was effectively transacted. It wasn't always elegant, but then neither was my door-to-door trek through St. Louis on my way to Congress. But it did represent the beautiful dance of Democracy, and the best way of managing common resources and settling differences of which I am aware.

I shudder to think of where we would be if a democratic republic had not taken hold and thrived in this country.

CHAPTER 3

The More Things Change...

As I suggested above, once having arrived on Capitol Hill and finding my way around the facilities, it didn't take long for the real action to unfold in earnest. In this chapter, I'd like to share a few experiences that marked my early tenure in Congress, each of which I believe bore enormous similarity, and therefore significant relevance, to the issues front and center today.

Among the most compelling of these were experiences involving such matters as our relationships with Russia, the Middle East, and the growing threat of terrorism. Also, domestic financial issues, such as management of the debt ceiling, controlling health-care costs, working toward fair international trade, and revising the tax code.

I believe that few would argue that these matters are not still prominent today.

When I read or hear the news today, I am often astonished at the degree to which the problems that drew our major attention during the first part of my Congressional career are the very same ones (albeit with modified contexts) that our current leaders are confronting. One might attribute this to our failure to resolve these issues back in the day; but I believe that this is the wrong conclusion to draw. Certain matters of great import are multi-generational or trans-generational in their resolution, while others require periodic revisiting under any and all circumstances. And finally, there are those in which ideal solutions are beyond the powers of humankind to achieve. These matters must be tackled perpetually if they are to be effectively addressed at all.

As an ambitious young member of the House, most of my efforts involved legislation initiatives. I would emphasize that the heavy lifting associated with the legislative process takes place within the committee structure. As mentioned at the end of the previous chapter, I was very fortunate within the early years of my tenure to obtain a seat on the House Ways and Means Committee — widely viewed as the committee that wields the most power over domestic affairs of any in the House of Representatives. Under the current structure, Congress features twenty committees with multiple sub-committees. Ways and Means, however, retains jurisdiction over such critical processes as management of the tax code, the federal budget, Medicare, trade relationships, and other aspects of government that are germane to the day-to-day lives of each and every American.

It is hardly a stretch to suggest that virtually everything that touches government passes in one form or another through the portal of Ways and Means.

It is within these committee frameworks that bills are written and modified, disputes are resolved, and legislation is drafted. Once a bill passes through the appropriate committee, in most cases, it has taken its approximate final form (though certainly incremental modifications can and do happen), and the legislation is put to a vote by the entire Congress. As is widely known, under typical protocols, once a bill is passed in the House it moves to the Senate where it may face further modifications. Subsequent to Senate passage, it is presented to the President for signature and execution.

At least that's the way it's supposed to work. Sometimes, it actually does follow this script.

Across the legislative process, long-standing protocols such as fair consideration and parliamentary procedure serve as essential guideposts. These concepts date back well before the formation of the United States. They originated in British Common Law and imply the obligation of Congress to ensure that the viewpoints of all parties impacted by a bill have been received and that all members have an opportunity to voice their perspectives.

Protocols form the essence of the legislative process, but they are nuanced, idiosyncratic, and complicated. Under the best of circumstances, it takes a while to understand them. Knowing, for instance, when you can and cannot not speak, when and whether the Committee Chair would be likely to recognize you, etc., is a very formidable, time-consuming challenge. And, in addition, it is important to understand the mood of the chamber—who is friendly, who is hostile to you, and at what level of intensity. Also, their depth of understanding of the prevailing issue or bill presented to them any given time. Until one has mastered these subtleties, it is difficult if not impossible to be an effective member of Congress.

One of the earliest, most impactful subjects with which I tackled and dealt was the Debt Ceiling — an issue that plagues us to the present day. As a matter of law, a limit to the aggregate indebtedness of the United States is a relatively new concept. It first appeared in the statutes in 1917, in part as a means of financing our entrance into the First World War (we entered the war in April of that year). Ironically, in 1939, at the outset of the Second World War, Congress amended the governance language to account for all the debt accumulated by the Federal Government (it has previously applied exclusively to certain bonds, bills, and notes). Perhaps, not surprisingly, it required upward adjustments to its size in every year of that conflict.

At the time of my arrival in Washington, the process was such that the House would first pass a Budget Resolution to fund its operations. Then, if and when the stipulated funding amount required an expansion of the debt ceiling, Congress would vote on this issue separately.

Again, all of this fell under the portfolio of Ways and Means, which would lead the process of budgetary drafting and approval, and then whenever necessary (often) would drive the process to expand the debt limit. One way or another, and whether I volunteered or was anointed (I don't specifically recall), the job of persuading every member of Congress and especially Democrats, to lend their support devolved to me.

In the world of politics, this process is called whipping the votes. And so, whip the votes I did. There were upsides and downsides to this. Happily, I found it did offer opportunity for meeting a broad swath of my fellow Representatives and their staffs. On the other hand, whipping a Debt Ceiling Expansion bill was always a grueling, thankless task. From the point of view of a member of Congress, there's no upside to voting "Yes," as doing so you hold yourself open to being labeled a spendthrift — seeking to drive the populous into insolvency. Often when I met with caucus members, they'd tell me that they knew the expansion had to be approved, but believed that there were sufficient votes without them to enable them to achieve their ideal objective — a debt ceiling expansion which they themselves did not have to vote in.

However, everyone understood that the alternative was a failure to fund the appropriations approved by Congress itself. So ultimately, most of the members came around.

This was driven of course by the increasing magnitude of the limit — the quaint pittance that it represents of today's deficit notwithstanding. Speaker O'Neill gave me the honor of being the member in charge of this into perpetuity. Thus, I became "Congressman Debt Ceiling." I felt like I was being assigned Bathroom Cleanup Monitor duties at camp. The process was somewhat mechanical, the task certainly lacked the glamor of other assignments, and again, no member was happy to hear from you when you ask for a few minutes of his or her time to discuss the subject. But the issue was a serious one. Inflation was running rampant around that time, and again, by the standards of the era, the deficits were growing alarmingly large. It was important work with a great deal at stake.

"You seem to be good at it. You're working hard at it. You can explain it to Members and that will help get their vote. This is a matter of persuasion," I was informed by O'Neill. He was right. And it did expand my network of relationships within Congress.

I endured this exercise about ten times in the late seventies and early eighties, and, finally, I became fed up with the process (really all of Congress was fed up). I went back to the Speaker and to the Chairman of the Ways and Means Committee (by then overseen by the one and only Dan Rostenkowski, "Rosty") and said this is really a waste of time. Everybody knows that once Congress made a budget spending decision, it is implicitly approving a debt limit at the same time. I then suggested that we put forward legislation that whenever a budget resolution implied a breaching of the prevailing debt limit, the expansion of the debt ceiling would automatically be part of the process. Two bills, one vote. Much more efficient, right?

Both Tip and Rosty thought it was a good idea, and this founded the basis for what ultimately became the Gephardt Rule. Specifically, the rule stipulated that whenever the House passed a budget that required an expansion of the borrowing limit, a resolution for expansion would be included as part of the original budget package.

The Gephardt Rule passed, and I think it added great efficiency to the funding process. However, in 1994, in the aftermath of a mid-term election rout by the Republicans, the new Speaker, Newt Gingrich, led the enactment of The Contract for America—a wide-ranging set of reforms that actually took the form of a multitude of legislative actions, some of which passed and some that didn't. The Contract called for the elimination of the Gephardt Rule, and that part of it indeed passed. So, for the last generation, Congress has reverted to dealing with the debt limit independently of the budget process.

Oh, well, it had a good run while it lasted.

I hope that readers will forgive me here if I take the perverse pleasure of busting out the old phrase, "What goes around comes around." This past decade in particular, the issue of the Debt Ceiling has plagued the Federal Government, causing more than one initiation of a shutdown process. And the problem is getting worse across time. It is hardly a stretch to suggest that the national debt has spiraled out of control in recent years. As I see it, very little productivity has come out of a brinksmanship process that involves waiting until the statutory ceiling is reached. And then witnessing the two parties fighting like cats and dogs until the inevitable happens and the ceiling is expanded. Here's where it stops being amusing. If our elected representatives do not act assertively to fix this mess, one of these times around there's a fair likelihood that the United States will default on its debt. This would be an unimaginable failure of governance and one that could have dramatic, unforeseen consequences. If anyone in Congress wants to avoid this by dusting off the old Gephardt Rule, well, I'm available to advise them on its nuances.

A second major issue during my early tenure on Ways and Means involved President Carter's initiative to contain Health Care costs. Carter had placed Health Care reform at the center of the platform upon which he was elected in 1976. And the issue was central to his successful efforts to stave off a primary challenge from Ted Kennedy in 1980. Both gentlemen were passionate about the subject, but their approaches were discernably different. Essentially, Kennedy was angling for universal health insurance, which in current times is referred to as a "single payer" (i.e., the Federal Government) system. Though Senator Kennedy never achieved this "dream" (a term he actually used in his concession speech at the 1980 Democratic National Convention), Single Payer remains a primary objective of the country's current Progressive Movement.

Carter's approach, embodied in the "Hospital Cost Containment Act of 1977," was more incremental. In essence, the President proposed a statutory mandate on hospital expenditures. Then, as now, overall health-care costs were spiraling out of control. The problem continues to grow in terms of severity and importance. Each step up the cost ladder not only redounded to the detriment of the American Consumer, but also put an incremental strain on the Federal Government by virtue of the huge outlays required to fund programs such as Medicaid and Medicare.

The financing of these Governmental Health Care programs fell under the natural purview of Ways and Means, and, as anticipated, we perpetually allocated untold amounts of time and resources to the challenge of holding expenses down. But I felt that the bill, which sought to solve the problem by placing an arbitrary, federally mandated cap on what hospitals could charge for a given procedure, offered the wrong approach. And I opposed the legislation from the outset.

The bill was a very hotly debated from beginning to end. I came out against it because I believed that the root of the problem was not what hospitals were charging, but rather an inefficient relationship between the system and the patients it served. What I believe was needed — then and now — was a different set of incentives between patients and providers embodied in the health-care management system. The system paid providers for procedures rather than delivering the most cost-efficient health services for the customer-patient —same as today.

In the late 1970s, approximately 85 percent of Health Care expenditures involved the patient and primary physician relationship, taking such forms as co-payments and deductibles that reside outside of the coverage umbrella for health insurance. The percentage has dropped a bit over the decades and now stands at about 75 percent, but part of the reason for this is that the average length of a visit to a primary care physician is now less than fifteen minutes. Moreover, according to government estimates, a significant percentage of the populous — approximately 28 percent of men and 17 percent of women — do not have a primary physician at all.

Because of this, hospital emergency rooms serve as the primary care mechanism for a significant portion of the population. While this was and remains a problem to this day, even back in 1977 it made no sense to set an arbitrary limit on hospital expenditures. In addition, among the outgrowths of the enormous socioeconomic diversity that we enjoy in this country, different regions, municipalities, and even neighborhoods have widely divergent health-care dynamics and cost profiles rendering the setting of caps even more problematic.

My opposition to the bill put me in hot water with the White House and Democrats in both the House and the Senate. I knew I was going against the grain, but I believed I was right. And, my opposition led to the consideration of alternative solutions, including those involving outreach to doctors, hospital officials, and other members of the health-care community, in an effort to come up with a fair and more cost-effective rational pricing construct.

Of course, these issues continue to vex us to the present day, and as the American population ages it will grow in magnitude and proportion in the future. The role of government in the funding and oversight of the Health Care system is about as controversial as any of the issues that currently confront us. Opinions across the spectrum could hardly be more divergent. Progressives feel that access to medical care is a basic human right that should be guaranteed by the government at levels of protection that would rise to those contained in the Bill of Rights. Conservatives wish to unleash market forces as the core of their solution. And this implies a diminished role for government.

Both sides are entrenched in their views, and the typical citizen can be justified for not knowing what to think. For me, these transformational challenges are best managed through the political vetting process that is the theme of this book. It is incumbent upon those who, for example, advocate "Medicare for All" to make their case in such a way as to convince most of the electorate as to the wisdom of this position. The other side faces the same dilemma.

And neither side in this debate has addressed factors which actually cause most of the chronic conditions we face as we age — diabetes, cancer and cardiovascular problems. Our healthcare system is arguably the best in the world at treating and managing chronic diseases but is failing to effectively help people to prevent the symptoms of poor health status from occurring in the first place.

So America's healthcare costs now are nearly 20% of GDP. Managing these chronic conditions is very expensive and that doesn't ever confront the poor quality of life people with these conditions experience. Healthcare experts think the percentage of GDP consumed by health costs will be 40% in the foreseeable future. So if we can't do better on preventing chronic diseases these costs will break the bank.

However, although time consuming and inefficient, the mechanisms of "democratic republic" governance (the vetting and advancing of laws through a legislature, the enactment and enforcement of these laws overseen by an Executive Branch, and the entire construct under perpetual review by an independent judiciary) are, I believe, far and away our best bet for getting to the right answers.

So far, that process has produced today what is a sound and effective compromise regarding healthcare for our older citizens (Medicare), our low income citizens (Medicaid) and our citizens who are just above average poverty rates (the Accountable Care Act).

And these three programs represent a very effective partnership between Federal and State governments and the private sector. In all of these programs the health benefit is primarily provided by the private sector and most of the money to pay for those benefits comes from the public sector.

So the long, frustrating process of democracy has provided a solution that has governments providing a most important service for people who have struggled or failed to provide it for themselves. However, the service is provided by the private sector which has a better performance than government in providing a cost efficient quality service for people.

The long debate over who should pay for health coverage for millions of Americans and who is best to deliver that coverage has been settled (for now). Still to be settled is how can the public and private sector working together deliver a better healthcare product that reduces overall costs while simultaneously improving the health status of most Americans.

It is worth noting here that it has taken 60 years for democratic governance to settle the healthcare questions surrounding who pays and who is best equipped to deliver healthcare services. Hopefully, it won't take another 60 years to figure out how to improve the product so we reduce costs and improve health status at the same time.

As slow and frustrating as progress in this area has been, it would be far, far worse if the decisions were being made by one person instead of 535.

During this same period of my early days in Congress, I made two official trips to foreign lands, both of which were quite astonishing as they unfolded. And I believe both had an uncanny element of foreshadowing of the foreign policy challenges of the present day.

The first was a trip to the Union of Soviet Socialist Republics (USSR), which was the official name of what is otherwise known as Russia from the time of the Russian Revolution all the way through to the collapse of the communist regime around 1990. The year was 1979, and the trip was led by the House Whip, John Brademas, who represented Indiana's Third District (which includes the campus of the University of Notre Dame). He was a naval veteran of the Second World War, held degrees from Harvard and Oxford, and after the conclusion of his political career became President of New York University. John led a delegation of about twenty of us to Moscow where we visited the Duma (the Soviet Senate) and met various government leaders under the autocratic regime of Leonid Brezhnev. It was a fascinating experience.

Our trip also included a visit to St. Petersburg (then called Leningrad) and Armenia, now a pseudo independent nation but then part of the Soviet Union nestled on the Eastern Boarder of Turkey between the Baltic and Caspian Seas. We were watched very closely by multiple officials whose job it was to "host" each of us, and, more importantly, to monitor our affairs.

During our ride through Armenia together, one of my senior guides told me that neither he nor any of his colleagues in the Duma ever visited the region. "You know, we are a long way from Moscow," he said (approximately 1,100 miles). He went on to point out that Armenia was near areas with the highest concentration of Muslims in the Soviet Union. Further, he said that the entire Soviet leadership felt that the prospect of Islamic provinces asserting themselves in non-secular ways was their biggest worry. He predicted great unrest and political revolutions.

Eventually he stated that the problem would be an enormous one for the United States as well.

Upon our return to Moscow — and on the last night of the trip — the Soviet leadership invited each member of the delegation to dine at the home of a senior government official. My host that night was General Viktor Paputin, the Director of the Interior. This evoked images of oversight of national parks and such. However, as I learned during my visit to his home, his primary role was to supervise the Gulags, or prisons. He was short, stocky, and highly gregarious. His walls were adorned by moose and deer heads — trophies of his hunting exploits.

My own hunting experience was limited to rabbits and other small mammals, but he encouraged me to migrate to big game. One way or another, we bonded over the sport.

The dinner party consisted of General Paputin and his three daughters and their husbands, each of whom was a senior Communist Party official. There was a bottle of authentic Russian vodka in front of each man's plate (the women weren't invited to imbibe). The menu of six or seven courses was ushered in by a "bottoms up" toast by each member of the gathering. Paputin gave the first toast and was very eloquent. I was scheduled to give the last one, but when the time came, I wasn't in very good shape. I'd never been drunk in my entire life, but I got through it.

We exchanged books at our parting, and I think the dinner was success overall.

The next morning was the farewell meeting, and though I was quite hung over, I was determined to get there on time. General Paputin, however, did not — he showed up around noon wearing sunglasses. The trip took place in April, and it was much to my shock when I read in the New York Times in early December that he had been shot and killed in Afghanistan.

General Paputin's mission in that country had been to join a group of KGB officials in some final diplomatic efforts to avoid war. From the outset, it didn't go as planned, and several people on Soviet side — including Paputin's entire visiting contingent — were killed within the first week.

Shortly thereafter, the Soviets launched a full-scale invasion of the country, and the rest, as they say, is history.

As all of this was unfolding, I was interacting a great deal with my colleague Charlie Wilson, an Annapolis Graduate, Navy veteran, and former senior official in the Defense Department. Charlie was on the Appropriations Committee and was responsible for, among other thing, oversight of military expenditures. He was a guy with a great interest and expertise in military affairs and was at the time working closely with the CIA, which in turn was naturally immersed in dealing with the Afghan situation.

When the Soviets finally withdrew from Afghanistan in 1989, everyone in Washington was pleased with the outcome. At this time, Charlie was adamant that we not depart militarily from the region, lest it descend into terrorism. This was his political position, but he lost the battle.

Of course, years later, Osama bin Laden set up partially backed Saudi operations in Afghan territory. Everyone knows what that incident precipitated. The Saudis, like many players on the world stage, were working both sides of the equation. They have been our allies for many decades but will almost always hedge their bets by giving money to interests that are hostile to the Saudi Royal family and United States.

All of which brings me to the other major foreign sojourn I undertook during this period: an expedition to Saudi Arabia. The trip took place in late 1979 and featured only a very small contingent, which was led by G. William Miller, who served as Secretary of Treasury and later as Federal Reserve Board Chairman. But at the time of this excursion, he had just been appointed Treasury Secretary. (Miller is the first person in U.S. history to serve as both Fed Chair and Treasury Secretary. The second is Janet Yellen.) The only other member in attendance were Congressman Jim Leach, a Republican from Iowa who was a distinguished expert in foreign affairs, and of course yours truly.

The trip took place amid the energy crisis, a time when Americans were struggling with huge oil price increases and lines at the pump. Our mission was to encourage the Saudis to increase production. Part of our itinerary included what we believed at the time to be a mostly ceremonial introduction to His Royal Highness, King Khalid. Our guide on this journey was the former Governor of South Carolina and U.S. Ambassador to Saudi Arabia, John C. West. Before we arrived at the palace in Riyadh, Ambassador West took great pains to inform us that the visit would be brief and managed under long-standing protocols for such meetings. He did not expect the visit to last more than five or ten minutes.

Upon arrival, we had expected a brief audience with the King and a small group of advisors. Instead, we encountered the entire Royal Family, all standing in a line against the wall. As many of you are no doubt aware, Saudi Royalty is highly prolific. King Khalid had about ten children, and, in addition, there was a large contingent of what must have been spouses, nieces, nephews, etc.

Through an interpreter, the King spoke to us for an entire hour about a recent terrorist invasion of the Masjid Al Haram, the holiest mosque in that holiest of Islamic cities: Mecca. In late November of 1979, rebel forces had seized the mosque, and about a thousand people were killed in the action. The Saudi Government, in conjunction with French and various regional allies, surrounded the facility and began a siege that lasted more than two weeks. In early December, Saudi forces recaptured Masjid and arrested and then summarily beheaded sixty-seven of the militant invaders.

Upon hearing these details, Ambassador West was speechless. He had been aware of the invasion and the siege, but until that time did not understand their significance to the King and to the world at large. It was, in fact, earthshaking, and the King was particularly adamant in telling us that he believed that his highest calling as a leader in the Islamic world was to protect the sanctity of these holy places.

"And we failed," he told us, vowing that it could never happen again. We departed with a clear understanding of the gravity of these issues and his motivation to address them.

As fate would have it, the seizure of Masjid Al Haram transpired just two short weeks after radical Islamic extremists took possession of the U.S. Embassy in Tehran, where fifty-two Americans were held against their will for 444 days. Iranian Leader Ayatollah Ruhollah Khomeini announced the discharge of these hostages exactly one year after their seizure on November 4, 1980 — the day that Ronald

Reagan defeated Jimmy Carter to become the 39th President of the United States. Their actual release came on January 20, 1981, the day of Reagan's inauguration.

The message — from the Ayatollah to outgoing President Carter and America — could not have been more plainly delivered.

As King Khalid addressed us, there was little doubt in my mind that the Iranian and American hostage crisis was prominent in his thoughts. Events spiraled out in web-like fashion from there, with the Saudis sending aid to all parts of the Islamic world and the emergence of a global problem that crescendoed into catastrophes like the September 11, 2001 terrorist destruction of the World Trade Center. Of course, these events continue to plague us, in ways large and small, up to the present day.

In terms of current foreign policy, I find that to an eerie extent while so much has changed over the past forty-odd years, much remains the same. The Soviet Union has gone back to the future and is Russia. Leningrad is St. Petersburg once again, but Moscow is still Moscow, and the Bear remains an easily angered, dangerous, and perplexing beast. Over the past decade, Russia has reasserted its expansionary proclivities, most visibly in proximate regions such as Crimea and the Ukraine. The country, while nominally a democracy, is ruled by the iron will of one man — President Vladimir Putin. As has been the case for centuries, enemies of the ruling regime risk and often experience violent death. Putin has played a complicated game of three-dimensional chess with us in the Middle East taking among other forms, his support of Syria's genocidal regime under Bashar al Assad.

Perhaps more prominently, the discouraging, vexing issue of Russian interference into the 2016 U.S. Presidential Election has become a multi-year, debilitating obsession in this country. And as I write this book, more questions remain than answers. The nation is polarized between those who believe that the Trump Campaign colluded with Russian agents to rig the outcome, and those that believe the whole episode was a farcical witch hunt perpetrated by Washington insiders.

But everyone agrees on one thing (which is also the uniform conclusion of all the investigations that have taken place): the Russians most certainly expended material resources to influence and disrupt our electoral processes in the year 2016. Russia is intent on doing everything it can to divide and polarize the American people.

I cannot complete this story about Russia without describing the great hope all of us had after the Berlin Wall fell in 1989 that Russia could finally transition to be a democratic and capitalist country for the first time ever.

In fact I went to Russia a number of times in the nineties with my Republican counterpart, Newt Gingrich, to offer help to the Russians to be able to make this transition.

On one of the visits, after speaking with Boris Yeltsin and other top leaders, I sent a message to President Bill Clinton and urged him to bring Russia into NATO — sooner than later. President Clinton tried hard to do that but for a lot of complicated reasons that never came about. So since 2000 Russia and the world has been stuck with Vladimir Putin. In retrospect, all of our efforts to help Russia to make that transition were a missed opportunity. Fundamental change in governance is always difficult and slow to achieve. My only hope is that some point in the future Russia will get to democracy instead of a failed authoritarian model.

Somehow, the House of Saud endures in Saudi Arabia under the reign of current King Salman. His son and heir apparent, Crown Prince

Mohammed bin Salman, is one of the most influential and controversial actors on the world stage. Enemies of the regime disappear into thin air. One way or another, the Saudis remain important to us — their region and the world — because of their large oil resources. But Islamic unrest persists, and in some areas, thrives. U.S. forces are perpetually deployed in defensive actions and, more recently, in mostly successful efforts to destroy the regional Caliphate — makeshift Islamic nations that typically traverse recognized national borders. With the Saudis, perhaps the best we can hope for is that they can modernize their country and reduce the importance of their radical religious element.

Unfortunately, it can be argued that we've made scant progress in finding sustainable solutions to many of the same problems in which I was involved in my early days in the House. I have no profound insight to offer in solving these problems and unfortunately expect them to continue to wreak their havoc on world affairs for as far as one wishes to gaze into the future. If I had any message to convey at all respecting these topics, it is the need to perpetually recommit and reinvest in global diplomacy.

And I want to emphasize the importance of using our governance structures to gather intelligence, identify problems, and respond in the most rational, feasible manner, to issues that inexorably arise beyond our borders. Attempting to encourage nation building in countries that have no experience in self-government has proven very difficult if not impossible. Our experience in Japan and Germany after the Second World War may have led us into believing nation building is possible and even easy.

But somehow we managed to survive various crises of the late seventies. As mentioned above, Carter lost to Reagan, and this ushered in a new governance construct in Washington. Reagan's impressive 1980 victory put him in the White House and also flipped the Senate, which going into the election featured a 58 to 41 Democratic majority (Harry Flood Byrd, Jr. of Virginia had been a lifelong Democrat, but ran and served as an Independent from 1970 to 1982). That morphed into a 53 to 46 post-election split in favor of the Republicans. My party also lost over thirty seats in the House during that election cycle, but still reserved a healthy majority of 243 to 192. Tip O'Neill retained his post as Speaker of the House, and as history shows, went on to enjoy a combative, lively, but on-balance highly productive relationship with Ronald Reagan in the White House.

I was privileged to have a front row seat and a routinely active role in this dynamic. At this point, I'd like to review two pieces of bi-partisan legislation in which I was involved at the time, and which still bear an enormous degree of resonance today.

The first falls under the heading of foreign trade — an issue that remains front and center in today's roster of challenges. My interest in this area was driven in significant part by what I was hearing back home in St. Louis. My constituents were deeply concerned about the loss of manufacturing jobs — autos and beyond — to unfair trading practices by the Japanese. The general feeling was that due to the lower standards and cost of living in that country and its neighbors, Japanese corporations were able to produce their goods at much lower costs than those of the United States and to pass these savings onto buyers in the form of lower prices.

In addition, the considerably lower bar that existed in these jurisdictions in terms of environmental, safety, and workers' rights laws further tilted the playing field against American manufacturing. This was a period when Americans were beginning to feel the full force of competition in auto sales from Japan. For the first time in automotive history, Toyotas and Hondas were competing for domestic road space with Fords and Chevys.

Other elements of American commercial disadvantage in international trade took such forms as downward manipulation of their currencies and dumping — a practice under which a company or country chooses to export products at a deeply discounted price (often below the cost of production) as a means of protecting domestic markets.

One way or another, the American trade deficit was growing by leaps and bounds at the time. For most of the 1960s and into the 1970s, the United States operated at a trade surplus — exporting more than we imported. By the time of my arrival in Congress, the tide had reversed. Between 1975 and 1976, we went from a $12 billion surplus to a $6 billion deficit. At the close of decade (and in part due to the formation of OPEC), the negative trade balance had risen to nearly $30 billion. Of course, these figures are a quaint anachronism relative to today's numbers, which now routinely run into the hundreds of billions. But it was nonetheless a matter of grave concern at the time.

I took on this issue directly. There were already laws on the books against the above-mentioned dumping process. But I felt that we should attack the problem more comprehensively. This was the genesis of a piece of legislation called the Gephardt Amendment. Its goal was to attempt to create a more level playing field for international trade by seeking to ensure that companies had similar rules of engagement for marketing their products internationally.

Its primary target was Japan, with whom we then had the largest imbalance (since supplanted by China). But Japan is a notoriously difficult country for foreign corporations to market their products. Auto exports, for instance, are nearly impossible to sell to the Land of the Rising Sun.

Therefore, I aimed the legislation at trying to break down foreign trade barriers in countries like Japan. My proposal was such that every country that imposed visible material barriers to the sale of our products would either need to modify them or face tariffs on their exports to the United States. I was less concerned with the actual amounts of exports that we generated and focused on the removal of barriers and the reasonable rules of engagement. Under these circumstances, if our products were treated with fairness in the global marketplace, we would be certain to reduce the deficit and help American production and workers in the process.

The bill was — to say the least — controversial. I knew at the outset that my approach was rather simplistic and that the globalization of trade (commerce across land masses and oceans, between nations of different cultures, resources, and modes of operation) was and will always be complicated and problematic. There will always be winners and losers and solving one problem will invariably from time-to-time lead to the creation of others.

These issues are more complicated as the miles between trade partners increase, as do the different natures of national comportment, legal systems, and socioeconomic structures. Striking deals with countries like Canada or those in Western Europe is comparatively easy.

These are nations with which we share many similarities. Engaging efficiently with governments in Asia-Pacific, Africa or the Middle East is a different matter entirely. In these more distant realms where the rule of law may take significantly different interpretations than those we hold, and where they don't enforce the concept of Intellectual Property, we are compelled to adopt a more nuanced approach and often settle for imperfect solutions.

Everyone is for free trade, provided it is defined under their own terms. And, of course, these terms differ between countries and even among individuals. As I would tell my constituents when the issue arose: the best we could hope for is fair trade — a fair shake. Under those circumstances, we are doing right by our business and workers, and that's about the best we can do in our jobs as government officials.

By way of background, the basis upon which we sought to attack these issues was the General Agreement on Tariff and Trade (GATT). Originally signed shortly after the Second World War (October 1947), its goal was to minimize international trade barriers by eliminating or reducing tariffs, quotas, and subsidies while preserving important and rational, governing regulations.

However, GATT, as a matter of necessity, was an agreement that required solving for a low common denominator — identifying that subset of protocols upon which the participating counties could agree. This both narrowed its scope and reduced the number of participants — in 1947 only twenty-three nations signed on to the initial agreement. To put this in perspective, GATT's successor enterprise, the World Trade Organization (WTO), founded in January 1995, featured participation by 159 countries.

However, an agreement between more than one hundred nations demands an even lower common denominator than did the twenty-three-nation GATT framework. For this reason, we have entered into superseding bi-lateral or multi-lateral trade agreements, such as the North American accord known as NAFTA. Even as President Clinton's Majority Leader in the House in 1993 I opposed approving the NAFTA agreement we were presented with then. My opposition stemmed from a lack of provisions in the Treaty to push Mexico to better enforce its labor and environmental laws. Since then, Democratic legislators have pushed our trade negotiators to get bilateral trade treaties that do achieve greater compatibility between our labor and environmental laws and practices and the trading partner involved. Although the Trump Administration withdrew from NAFTA, the agreement represented the kind of workable arrangement that is difficult to create on the world stage.

The Gephardt Amendment was an aggressive concept, mandating reduction in trade deficits by forcing reform on our trading partners who enjoyed the largest surplus with us. It was attacked as being overly protectionist, and in retrospect, this critique is probably accurate. It had bi-partisan support, but ultimately it failed on the floor. However, it re-emerged as a centerpiece of a piece of legislation called the Omnibus Trade Foreign Trade and Competitiveness Act of 1988. It was signed into law in the summer of that year, about six months before the expiration of President Reagan's second term. President Clinton renewed it twice.

Trade issues continue to plague us and probably will forever. The ideal — free and fair trade across all countries with minimal disruption to trade flows — is next to impossible to achieve in the foreseeable future. Nonetheless, working diligently toward that goal is an imperative. History shows that a robust global trade framework improves the lot of Americans and of all humanity. In our increasingly connected, interdependent world, trade must increase; a reduction would be unthinkable.

The role of Congress in all of this is indispensable. And again, I emphasize that a representative government featuring 535 legislators, as supported and balanced by the Executive Branch, is a far superior framework than allowing a single person or a handful of unaccountable individuals to make these decisions on our behalf. Our trade agreements thus, rightly, and justifiably, run through Congress.

I am particularly pleased with the outcomes we achieved with the Japanese. Today, three out of every four Japanese cars sold in the United States are built in North America. In 2015, U.S. workers in Japanese auto plants pumped out nearly four million vehicles, with over

10 percent of them actually exported. Japanese automakers employed nearly 100,000 direct workers, with another 375,000 working at dealerships in this country. It's a big change from where we began our trade efforts. In the 1970s, virtually all trade between the two nations involved us importing from them. I believe that this a shining example of what can be accomplished through bi-partisan legislative efforts, be they related to international trade or other matters.

As I mentioned earlier, most of the hard work is carried out in committees assigned to a given issue. Members of these committees are expected to have conducted thorough due diligence on all matters that fall under their purview. Representatives of the House Energy and Commerce Committee, for instance, which has operated under continuous fashion (albeit under different names) since the Washington Administration, can only conduct their business under the framework of a thorough understanding of the production, finance, consumption, technology, and other aspects of the energy sector. Through this wisdom, they bring bills to the floor; but the 435-member House of Representatives cannot be expected to have thorough knowledge of every potential law upon which it must vote.

In a typical year, more than 2,000 bills, and sometimes as many as 4,000, are presented to Congress, and, typically, only a small percentage (maybe 10 percent) are approved. And here it is important to bear in mind that the entire Congressional year is limited to 138 days when members are present and accountable to cast their votes. By the sheer math, a typical representative might be asked to cast ten or more votes on any given day and again cannot possibly be fully informed as to the details and merits of each of them.

To make matters more complicated, a disproportionate amount of legislative action is crammed into smaller periods before holiday recesses – in advance of factors such as budget deadlines, and, most acutely, at the end of the Congressional Calendar Year (Congress typically adjourns for the year a couple of weeks before Christmas).

The percentage of actual legislative acts that are enacted is much smaller as any bill that does receive Congressional approval is then passed on to the Senate, which may or may not choose to approve it, but whose approval is mandatory under our constitutional framework. Then it goes to the President's desk, and it is his or her prerogative to veto it — an action which requires a two-third majority of both houses of Congress to over-ride this action. The deliberate, time-consuming nature of the framework is part of the vision of the framers of the Constitution.

They wanted to avoid caprice and ensure deliberation. Consensus and compromise are and always will be the wages of legislative action.

The process takes a great deal of time and effort. It must be led by the informed and energetic efforts of one or more members of a committee bearing oversight responsibility for the area of focus. They then must do the hard work of informing the broader membership and advocate for their vote.

As one illustration of this, I'll wind the clock back a few years to 1982 and 1983 to my own efforts to enact a sweeping tax reform bill. It didn't pass until 1986, but here I am getting ahead of myself.

I began to focus on the tax code — particularly its mind-boggling complexity and the special advantages it bestowed on a favored view — in the early part of the 1980s. As a member of Ways and Means, this was a natural part of my responsibilities, and I found a kindred spirit in New Jersey Senator Bill Bradley. Like several others in Congress, Bradley was a famous athlete before entering the realm of politics, having been an All-American basketball player at Princeton, and then moving on to enjoy a Hall of Fame career in the NBA with the New York Knicks.

Bradley was a natural politician and very politically active even during his professional basketball career. No one was surprised when he ran for Senate in New Jersey shortly after his retirement. He won his seat in 1978 and served with distinction for three terms. But he was a born and bred Missourian, hailing from my very own district of Jefferson County.

We became lifelong friends and shared many common political concerns and viewpoints. He served on the Senate Finance Committee, which is the Upper Chamber's opposite number to Ways and Means. Soon enough, he and I began a series of discussions about reforming the tax code.

This fostered the Genesis of the Bradley/Gephardt Bill, also called The Fair Tax Act. Our introductory work began in 1982 and was closely monitored by President Reagan, who was gearing up for his 1984 re-election campaign. We focused upon two specific and straightforward objectives: 1) the elimination of special interest provisions; and 2) the reduction of the base rate — particularly at its uppermost brackets. The more philosophical objectives were simplicity, clarity, and fairness. At the time we began the initiative, top earners were paying 70 percent to the Federal Government, and there were fifteen separate income brackets.

The number of special considerations were too many to count. Examples of the embedded inconsistencies include the mortgage interest and charitable contribution deductions, a reduced levy on capital gains, depreciation allowances for investment in plant and equipment, and other idiosyncrasies embedded in the tax code.

We wanted to eliminate these types of complexities and reduce the bracket tables from fifteen to three: 10 percent, 15 percent, and 25 percent. We accomplished all of that by eliminating all special interests.

It was also important that the bill be revenue neutral — that it brought in roughly the same amount of levies that the government would have collected under the existing tax code. We did all of this in the belief that the country was way too complicated to be handing out tax breaks that would have unforeseen consequences. Our North Star was simplicity and fairness.

I spent much of the next two years — with and without Senator Bradley — speaking to ordinary citizens and professional organizations in economics and accountancy to describe our vision of tax reform and to argue for its merits as an initiative that would strengthen the economy.

Among our objectives, we wanted to simplify the filing process to the point where a citizen need not hire an outside tax preparer (as was and still is the rage), and that the entire tax form should be tight enough to fit on a post card.

But I realized early on that the best chance for success would require passing the credit on to others. And the most logical recipient of credit in this situation was the Chairman of the Ways and Means Committee, the aforementioned Dan Rostenkowski. I met with Rosty and laid out my case. I told him that I was passionate about the issue and had been working my tail off selling it across the country. However, I told him, political success would be best insured if the bill had his imprimatur. He told me he didn't know a great deal about tax policy, but that he did know how to screw people.

He also told me he would help, and eventually he put his own name on the legislation. This gave us terrific traction. We received another huge boost through our collaboration with Republican Representative Jack Kemp, another former athlete (NFL Quarterback) made good in Congress. He had arranged for the passage of his own tax bill in 1981 — shortly after Reagan's first inauguration — co-sponsored by Delaware Senator William Roth. As they were Republicans, there were philosophical and content-based differences between our approach and theirs. But on balance, we found ourselves aiming at the same objective: a simple, fairer, more effective set of tax laws on the books.

And then we received a further assist, from Treasury Secretary James Baker, who told us we had the President's support. At that point, with bi-partisan backing in both houses of Congress and the endorsement of the President, it was a fairly straightforward exercise to bring the bill into law.

But it took more than four years. It was only in late October of 1986 that the bill was enacted. Untold hours of hard work had gone into it — the blood and sweat of many of the country's finest legislators. Nobody outside the process saw this side of it. It was a grueling, excruciating process, but it was a perfect example, soup to nuts, of what I believe to be the magic of the legislative process under the banner of the U.S. Constitution.

And I am exceedingly proud of the result: we lowered the top tax rate to 28 percent, reduced the number of brackets from fifteen to three, eliminated sixty billion in loopholes, and transferred a burden of approximately twenty-five billion dollars from individuals to corporations.

And critically, it was – as we had pledged – revenue neutral. In fact, from the time of its passage in late 1986, all the way through the end of the century, federal tax receipts actually increased each year.

In terms of deductions, some sacred cows, such as the home mortgage and charitable contribution exemptions, remained in place. But we did eliminate a lot of exemptive nonsense and set the template for tax policy for years to come.

Inevitably, however, as time went by, some of the old habits re-emerged. Slowly but surely, special interest groups managed to slip in their agendas into the tax code. And, as we wound the clock forward toward the present era, we found the code to be yet again a hot mess.

Favored groups have re-secured their special treatment and in part, due to this slippage, overall rates went up.

All of which brings us to what is referred to in certain quarters as the Trump Administration's signature achievement in his first years in office: The Tax Cuts and Jobs Act of 2017. There was some of the same spirit in this legislation that had characterized our efforts back in the mid-eighties, but there were also glaring differences in terms of approach and content. For one thing, the 2017 Act was passed at a time when the Presidency, Senate, and House were all controlled by Republicans. It featured absolutely no bipartisanship.

No Democratic member of the House or the Senate voted for the bill, and thirteen House Republicans actually opposed it.

Times are different now. Under the last three administrations (Biden, Trump, and Obama), it is my observation that in each case, the opposition party focused on impeding the President's platform more than at any time during my tenure in Congress. I want everyone to understand that whatever else transpires in the future respecting these dynamics, hyper-partisanship is counterproductive and leads to inefficiencies in the legislative process—or to do nothing at all.

Bad bills get rammed through and good ones go begging. A lot of time and effort is wasted in the exercise of unilateral opposition.

But the level of partisanship associated with the two tax bills was only one component of the factors that separate them. The other most prominent one was the distribution of cost and benefit. Our bill in 1986 was clearly constructed as relief for the individual taxpayer and actually came at the expense of corporations and special interests. By contrast, the Tax Act of 2017 was explicitly framed to provide relief in the realm of corporate taxation. A good argument for that was the competitive disadvantage our corporations faced with rates higher than in most competitive developed countries.

But the final 2017 tax legislations suffered from being produced by a partisan coalition. Now, as Democrats have regained a majority, they have tried to reverse the 2017 bill with only their votes.

It is a matter almost beyond dispute that tax debates will persist for as long as societies can continue to organize themselves under forms of democratic governance. And, as I put my musings to writing, these disputes assume an increasingly dire sense of urgency. Of course, we've been through this sort of thing before — dating all the way back to the American Revolution, which was catalyzed by colonial dissatisfaction over the concept of taxation without representation. Indeed, it is hardly a stretch to suggest that throughout the course of recorded history, rebellions and wars have ensued over disagreements as to how much revenue a governing body can extract from its citizens and for what purposes.

Presently, many in both parties have become alarmed at the size of the Federal deficit — the direct result of government spending that has occurred without offsetting tax revenues. At the point of publication of this book, the National Debt is approximately $30 trillion and growing every day. And this doesn't even count the enormous contingent liabilities associated with Social Security and Medicare, which some studies estimate to be equal to or larger than the National Debt itself.

During my time in Congress, we attempted to tackle all these issues. Almost certainly, none of our answers were met to the complete satisfaction of everyone. But every effort we made was bipartisan in nature with the clear objective of finding solutions that would allow the country to remain united and to move forward together.

Tax policy was the hardest thing I worked on in my congressional career. And I was proud of not only the results, but of the way these efforts unfolded — honoring, at all times, the Majesty of Democracy, achieving resolutions through non-violent means, and working for the benefit of all citizens.

I close this chapter with my observation that the more things change, the more they indeed remain the same. As a rising young Congressman, I was thrust into issues described above, including foreign policy matters pertaining to countries such as Russia and those in the Middle East. Then, as now, Radical Islamic political activity (and, it must be said, terrorism) were alarming and growing plagues on our peace of mind. After the Wall fell in 1989, we hoped Russia was going to struggle toward achieving democracy and capitalism and even become a part of NATO. Now, we know they have returned to their past and changing the country may be an impossibility.

On the economic side of the equation, my peers and I attacked challenges ranging from trade wars, tax code improvement, debt ceilings, and the management of rising health-care costs.

Does any of this sound familiar?

Well, you bet it does, because, to borrow from Jefferson, "In the course of human events," yesterday's problems, the issues of the day, and the challenges of the future, all carry a common thread through them: the heartbeat of humanity.

As was the case in the past, we can only hope to address them through the imperfect consensuses brought out, with all their inefficiencies, through a framework that features rule making by the consent of the governed.

CHAPTER 4

Caucus Chair: An Exercise in Cooperation, Coordination, and Consensus

As I have already described, I made it to the U.S. House of Representatives and do not believe I spent my time there idly. For better or worse, and from the outset, I had the honor of being thrown right into the midst of the action.

In the mid-1980s, a pathway was emerging for me to climb higher on the Ladder of Legislative Leadership and I followed that path. I do not believe that I took this course from an outsized sense of personal ambition. I was in Congress, had fought hard to earn my seat, and tried to do my best for my constituents and the nation.

And there was more to do. I was burning with an energy to get things done. Ultimately, this form of determination led me to two (unsuccessful) presidential runs and to a long stretch as the Democratic Leader in Congress.

In this chapter, I wish to stress above all else the importance of open-mindedness, collaboration, and compromise in the legislative process. A true measure of success from this perspective is the level of bipartisanship that underlies any law-making dynamic. As I will re-emphasize later in the chapter, my experience is that without bipartisan cooperation, very little of importance can be achieved in a democratic republic such as ours.

But the next step in my journey is entirely partisan in nature. After the1984 election (in which Ronald Reagan crushed Walter Mondale) opportunity materialized for me to serve as Chairman of the Democratic Congressional Caucus. This was not a goal that I specifically set for myself. It was simply an outcome that derived from my efforts and commitment to the legislative progression.

Earlier on in this narrative, I mentioned some great mentors, including — perhaps most notably — Richard Bolling, a fellow Missourian, Second World War Combat Veteran, and a man who had a great influence on my life and political career. Dick took me under his wing, spoke to me nearly every day, and educated me on the workings of the House, Senate, and Presidency. He was smart as a whip and as tough as nails.

The Chair of the House Democratic Caucus was a gentleman named Gillis Long, another Second World War veteran and a member of the eponymous Louisiana political dynasty (Huey Long was his uncle). He was Bolling's best friend in the House, and (perhaps at Bolling's urging) he took a liking to me. Among other matters, he included me in an advisory group that was an important tool for him in managing the Caucus.

It was Gillis who first put the notion of seeking the House Caucus Chair into my head. It's the number three or four leadership position, surpassed only by the Speaker, Majority Leader, and Congressional Whip.

After my re-election in 1984, during which time I was working on the big tax bill with New Jersey's Bill Bradley, Gillis took me aside and suggested that I consider running as his successor.

Following this suggestion, I decided to put together a core organization of House members on the Democratic side who might support me in this effort. Some of the newer members — those who first came into the House with me in the '76 race — shared my views on several issues and agreed to be part of the Committee. Gillis not only was in my camp, but also brought along some older members, which was crucial to the success of the initiative. The rest of the task involved me working around the clock recruiting members for my committee. Happily, many of them agreed to join.

We immediately began convening as a group with an eye toward determining the most efficient path toward my winning the Chairmanship. I wasn't sure that I would be successful, but I was determined to try and would certainly have failed had I not had so many committed and able allies in this effort.

However, I wasn't the only member with an eye on the prize. One of my opponents was Ed Jenkins from Georgia, my seatmate in the Ways and Means Committee. He entered Congress the same year I did and was a guy I really liked. Perhaps more pertinently, he was from the South at a time when the Democratic Congressional contingent from that region was large, strong, cohesive, and essential. Having Gilis Long on my side (particularly as the incumbent to the position) was critical. It may have been the deciding factor and, obstacles notwithstanding, I won that election and became House Democratic Caucus Chair in early 1985.

Sadly, and coincidentally, Gillis died on January 20, 1985 — the day of the Second Reagan Inaugural.

As mentioned above, I assumed my duties as Caucus Chair at a time when there were an unusually large number of new members, many of them young, and all wanting to make a difference. It was an eager bunch, all wishing for seats on key committees, and all very desirous to utilize the Caucus as an agent for change.

One key objective was to increase the frequency of Caucus meetings, which was one of the main planks of my platform for Chair.

But there was a problem taking the human form of the larger-than-life Speaker of the House, Tip O'Neill. Tip wasn't a big fan of Caucus meetings. He felt that they were forums for disagreement and dissension within the Caucus.

I stayed on him. Virtually every week I'd meet with him and state my disagreement with his stance. "Mr. Speaker," I'd implore, "I really think you have nothing to lose by having more caucus meetings. We can find out what people think and where they're coming from on the various issues that we deal with. You could get updates from committee chairs on where they are and dealing with various pieces of legislation. And the only way you can avoid terrible disagreement is by communicating early, often, and transparently, and keeping everybody informed so that they felt they knew pretty much what was going on."

Eventually, I wore him down. He grudgingly agreed to allow a few more caucus meetings, but only up to a limit that fell short of my ambitions.

Such is the nature of political compromise. We did increase the frequency of meetings markedly from where it had been prior to that time. And what I learned in that process was that people — especially politicians — want information, which particularly in that context is power. It welds members together by rendering them informed on wide ranges of important subjects to which they otherwise might not have access.

Information also bestows confidence — that derives from being part of a group — and that increases their comfort as to the range and consequences of future outcomes.

Moreover, sharing information through multi-lateral communication — as transpires within caucus settings — allows for a better identification of core objectives, associated obstacles, and the nature of conflicts that might stand in the way of otherwise reaching a suitable legislative accord.

Back then, and as still applies today, members of the House were typically limited to two committee assignments. One of the problems with this is that, particularly for newer members, it is difficult to get a sense of what is going on inside other committees and they may have to vote yes or no on legislation from other committees.

The caucus framework thus gave members a much better sense of understanding as to the at-the-moment dynamics of the entire House at any given point in time. Beyond this, the sense of agency that members derived from being part of the group offered a huge benefit in setting a voting course on difficult, conflicting pieces of legislation. As Chairman, I found the forum to be invaluable, particularly any time I was impelled to "whip the vote" on budgetary matters or other problematic bills on the Congressional docket.

One primary example of this was the passage and management of the Clean Air Act and the Clean Water Acts. Originally enacted in 1970 (before my time in Congress), those bills were enormously complicated pieces of legislation, which required rigorous monitoring and multiple amendments, most notably those which were passed in 1977 and 1990. Leading this effort was Commerce Committee Chair John Dingell, a Michigan Democrat who at the point of his retirement in 2015 held the record for the longest tenure of any Congressman in American History (59 years).

Dingell's career was long and storied. But what I recall most was his ability to work within his committee on a bi-partisan basis. He listened to every member of the committee. Because of this, he was able to craft critical legislation and get it enacted, none in my view more important than Clean Air and Water Acts.

While the importance of this legislation is clear to everyone in the current age, it was very complicated and controversial in its passage. Younger readers may be less aware of this, but two generations ago it was not uncommon for actual fires to break out on Lake Erie. Other Great Lakes and major rivers were chockful of chemicals and pollutants.

I clearly remember flying out to Los Angeles for a political event in the late seventies and early eighties. Invariably, when you flew over the L.A. airport, you would notice a layer of brown smog over the entire city basin. The Greater Los Angeles Region has expanded dramatically since then in terms of population, road density, and other environmentally challenging factors, but brown smog is a relic of history. The Great Lakes, and most all the lakes and rivers in the country, are now largely free of the type of pollution that prevailed during our grandparents' day.

And it is substantially, in my view, because of the Clean Air and Water Acts.

Currently, acting as responsible custodians of the environment is an important issue across the political and commercial landscape. But I wish to remind everyone that it is not a new concern.

It was a vital part of the discourse, and ultimately the legislative agenda during my entire tenure in Congress (and beyond). It was a very complex challenge, one of the most difficult problems to navigate through the protocols of democratic governance. But everyone knew how important it was, and leaders from both sides of the aisle came together in an effort that I believe (among other things) sowed the seeds of the current environmental awareness.

All of this reinforced my commitment to caucus meetings, which became even more important in the wake of the 1980 election of Ronald Reagan. We were working on a great deal of important legislation at the time, and, because I didn't agree with much of the Gipper's legislative agenda, efficiency in our caucus became doubly important.

Yes, President Reagan and I differed on many political matters; but it was impossible not to like the man himself. I spent a lot of time in the White House during his time in office and could not help but form a deep admiration of him. He always led with humor and made everybody laugh. He was always a good listener; he responded to questions asked and concerns raised with respect; he never was angry, bitter, or difficult; and he treated people with human kindness and respect. I would say that no one in Congress — Democratic or Republican — that ever dealt with or worked with him came away from a meeting disliking him.

And another thing I have learned in politics through the years is that your "likability quotient" is a very important part of your ability to be a political leader.

President Reagan had it as much as anybody I've ever encountered.

It was around that time after I had become Caucus Chair that I thought that if you are going to advance the causes that stirred your passion, it was important to focus in on a small number of legislative objectives. I selected Health Care, Taxation, and Trade.

As discussed in an earlier chapter, I had opposed Jimmy Carter's hospital cost containment bill — a stance that drew a lot of anger and criticism from members of my own party, especially people inside the Carter Administration.

I believed, as one of the agents for the failure of that bill, that it fell to my lot to seek a suitable alternative. If I didn't like their suggestion,

I'd better come up with one of my own that might be more effective. So, during that period, I began working with David Stockman,
a Republican Congressman from Michigan who went on to become
Reagan's Office of Management and Budget (OMB) Director, on a piece
of health-care legislation that I thought made much more sense than
the Hospital Cost Containment Bill.

This is the Genesis of a piece of legislation called Gephardt
Stockman or (Stockman Gephardt), the objective of which was to
reduce health care costs by increasing market competition. Back then,
as is the case today, health expenses were an intractable problem. But
the nexus of the bill was to utilize the tax code to enable users of the
health-care system to choose price efficient alternatives for their medical needs. While health-care economics have experienced many twists
and turns since this initiative, suffice it to say that the effort was market-
based and bi-partisan.

My exertions on Tax Reform, also described in a preceding chapter, were long, frustrating, but ultimately successful—at least for a time
— due to my friendship and collaboration with Senator Bill Bradley.

We had a warm friendship across our time in Washington and
beyond, and, importantly, Senator Bradley was a member of the Senate
Finance Committee — the Upper Chamber's equivalent of Ways and
Means.

It took years, but ultimately passed, importantly, through a
bi-partisan effort. We received particular support from Reagan and
his Treasury Secretary James Baker. In addition to the assistance from
the Executive Branch, New York Congressman Jack Kemp was one of
our champions.

In essence the bill featured a wider tax base, the removal of
myriad loopholes, and a reduction in what was a maddening number

of tax brackets. I consider the effort to be a great success, and again, the key was bipartisanship.

I cannot — particularly in these conflicted times — overstate the importance of bi-partisan orientations in the legislative process. If you're going to put together a big legislative piece that's going to change something important — that is going to fundamentally alter the lives of your constituents — it really can't be done effectively unless different viewpoints and party orientations are represented. Moreover, if both parties are involved, the result is typically a superior piece of legislation than those enacted by a single party. This is neither a popular nor prevailing attitude in today's political environment; but I believe it is true, nonetheless.

I used to say to members of my caucus that none of us knows everything. I wish I did. I don't. Neither do you. Neither does anybody else. We've got to listen to one another, and learn from one another the things that we don't know but need to know to tackle some big problem we're working on together.

And that's what happened in that tax legislation. Now, I'd be the first to admit that the final product got watered down and changed in some ways with which I did not agree. But fundamentally, it was still a good product. It resulted in important modifications to the tax code. And that could only have happened if it was bipartisan process where there was lots of listening, working together, and making alterations so that we could bring on the votes to get the bill done.

The third piece of big legislation that I worked on in that period (1984 – 1986) was International Trade. It was naturally within my purview because my Ways and Means Committee had jurisdiction over trade. Beyond this, I had a deep sense that we were really being disadvantaged by our trade policies. Countries like Japan were enjoying access to a very open market in the United States — especially with automobiles and semiconductors — but without reciprocity in their markets

There were myriad reasons for the disparity, some of them legal, but many of them cultural. The American consumer culture is very open and interested in better products at a better price, no matter where they come from. Having visited Japan and speaking to informed sources, I quickly learned that their society was less open culturally to products from the outside.

One of the classic stories was that they wouldn't allow snow skis made in America or anywhere else. It was said that consumers there wouldn't buy foreign skis in Japan because they wouldn't work in Japanese snow. It's kind of a club in Japan, and I understand that.

But culture in a world economy makes it very difficult for other countries to compete on a fair basis. So, with that in mind, and seeing the alarming reduction in jobs in the United States auto industry (which is very important in the Midwest and in my district), I felt we needed to take strong action to try to level that playing field.

My view was simply this: yes, free trade, but it must be fair trade. My bill (a portion of a larger trade initiative with the provisions I'm discussing called the "Gephardt Amendment" was an aggressive means to get to that result. Essentially, it argued that if the trade deficit between the United States and any other country became materially distorted against us, the country that was abusing our trade privileges would be asked to adjust its policies to reduce that deficit. Further, their failure to do so would cause us to impose tariffs.

Simple, right?

Wrong. Tariffs are a blunt instrument, and the bill attracted a significant amount of harsh criticism, particularly from the business community and free trade advocates and adherents. And as the bill evolved, it was subject to inevitable dilution and modification

— perhaps appropriately so. In the end, its essence was reduced to investing more power in the President to enact tariffs.

It passed in 1987, and shortly thereafter, Ronald Reagan went to the Japanese and negotiated a reduction in the number of cars that would be exported into the United States. At minimum, it bent the curve of our trade deficit with that country, which in 2020 ($55.4 billion) was lower than it was in 1987 ($56.3 billion).

One outcome of this was unfortunately a significant slowing of the Japanese economy, which peaked in the early 1990s and has yet to recover. But another outcome was beneficial to the United States. In the 1990s, Japanese auto makers moved significant auto manufacturing facilities to the United States.

Today, when we think of trade imbalances, our focus is substantially on China; and rightfully so. President Trump enacted tariffs on the Chinese in 2018, and our issues with them remain at the forefront of our challenges. I would argue, though, that the steps we took to reign in the trade situation with Japan offered an informative roadmap as to how best to deal with these trials.

These were the building blocks for the next stages of my career. It was audacious at that time to think that a young member like me who had been in Congress for eight or nine years could even think of running for the Democratic nomination for president. But having served in a leadership position as Chair of the Democratic Caucus, and, more importantly, having brought forward some major initiatives on health care, taxation, and trade, I believed that I had a platform on which I could run. I also felt that I had the confidence of a lot of my colleagues, which is essential to even contemplate such an initiative.

As I considered this next bold move, I became increasingly convinced that the most important responsibility of a president was to work with Congress — day in and day out — to pass legislation needed in the country. Here, I owe a direct — but partially perverse — debt of gratitude to Jimmy Carter. I love him, thought he did many great things, and is certainly a wonderful human being.

But we all have strengths and weaknesses, and it struck me that his weakness was his inability to relate to the Congress. Part of that was just his thought process. He was an engineer and did not suffer fools gladly. Carter didn't want to sit in endless meetings to listen to people who he didn't agree with or weren't as competent as he was.

Part of this, in my opinion, was a lack of experience with Congress. He had been Governor of Georgia and had never been in Congress. I formed an opinion that such inexperience was a major handicap for any president. I really sensed that to be an effective president, it was essential to have some experience with Congress — working and listening with other members — and putting together the votes on a bipartisan basis that could move the country forward.

By 1985, I believed I could do that and that it would help guide me to a successful presidential bid and tenure in that great office. By 1988, I was ready to offer myself as a bi-partisan leader who could get things done the way they were intended: through cooperation, collaboration, coordination, and, above all, bi-partisanship.

The experience, if ultimately unsuccessful, was an essential one and it helped mold my entire life.

But all of that unfolds in the next chapter.

CHAPTER 5

Aiming Higher—My 1988 Presidential Run

My thoughts about taking a shot at the Presidency began shortly after the 1984 election when Walter Mondale lost by a monstrous margin to Ronald Reagan. At or near the top of my motivations were my observations, mentioned in the previous chapter, as to what I perceived to be President Carter's failure to work effectively with Congress.

I truly believed that I could forge the bipartisan agreements needed to solve or overcome big challenges. We do not have a parliamentary system of governance that has the chief executive in the role of leader of the parliament as well. I concluded our Presidential system would work much better if the President could be very effective in leading Congress.

By this time, I had observed his Ronald Reagan for four years. And even though he was a very likable fellow and really was a big unifier in the country, his efforts in dealing with Congress were, in my judgment, wanting. He was in some ways better than Carter in this realm, but he was neither in tune nor particularly interested in the details of legislation. For instance, he wasn't inclined to hold meaningful meetings with legislators, preferring to leave it to his aides (Jim

Baker in particular) to carry out the relatively unglamorous task of working out legislative compromises.

The Reagan Team was certainly competent in dealing with the House and Senate, but there was no substitute for the president directly managing the difficulties which would inevitably arise. With this in mind, and because of the frustration felt in Congress about its working relationship with the White House, I believed that my theme — a presidency that featured high interaction with the Senate and House — would draw a good deal of support from House members. That is where where I planned to begin my outreach.

So I began to ponder the mechanics of running for President. The first big step in the process is winning the party nomination, which in many ways is a more difficult task than winning the General Election. Unless you're an incumbent, you are likely to face off against any number of competent competitors in the primaries. In the General, you're up against a single opponent. However, at the same time as has been proven throughout history, the political positions you take to secure the nomination may at times be incompatible to those which optimizes your odds of winning the final race.

I started by reaching out to members of Jimmy Carter's political team, those who had secured him an improbable victory in 1976. These included Hamilton Jordan, who, after running the presidential campaign, served as Carter's Chief of Staff. I flew to Atlanta, mostly to pick his brain as to how I should proceed. I also met with Bill Romjue who had run Carter's Iowa campaign effort and launched him to the presidency. As an interesting and ironic aside, "Uncommitted" actually won Iowa by a wide margin, but Carter took second place and was on his way!

Then, as now, the path to the presidency starts in Iowa, the state which holds the first cycle of voting (in its case a caucus). Unless a candidate has enormous name recognition, personal wealth, a built-in constituency, or some combination thereof, the only way to win is through a long, sustained, on-the-ground effort.

As my plans continued to take shape, I also reached out to John Sears, a key advisor to winning and losing efforts on the Republican side for both Richard Nixon and Ronald Reagan.

Sears provided me with some invaluable advice. Among other elements of wisdom, he indicated to me that one of the biggest challenges I might face was retaining the attention of the press. He said the biggest problem for news organizations is that on most days there is nothing new happening to report, so they are constantly looking for anything new or different to report. On any given day leading up to an election, they are looking for new angles. It is essential to keep them engaged, but they constantly need new material — speaking to them repeatedly about the same subjects just won't cut it.

So, after speaking to a wide range of political people, I decided to travel with Bill Romjue to Iowa to get the lay of the land and to meet people in the state. I'd fly out, typically on a Thursday night, and spend the weekend traversing the Great State of Iowa — from Sioux City to Dubuque — meeting with Democratic County groups.

It was a bit reminiscent of the type of door-to-door campaign that got me to Congress — a shoe leather campaign — if you will. It's an approach that I believe matched well with my skills and disposition. I have always been able to relate and listen to people in a way that shows respect. That's what I did in Iowa.

Another advantage I thought I might have was that Iowa was adjacent to my home state of Missouri. Both were highly agricultural, with farming and food production comprising a significant portion of their economies. As such, I felt I had some familiarity with the issues most important to the state and the region.

I brought on a staff person, Jim Hawley, to help me develop a good agriculture policy proposal that I intended to feature — along with Tax and Health Care Reform — as centerpieces of my platform.

As my activity in the Hawkeye State took hold, I realized that I must also set up a similar effort in New Hampshire. New Hampshire was the second state in the nomination sequence and held a bona fide primary. The distinction between the two forms of voting was significant. While caucuses such as those held in states like Iowa involved a concentrated and limited number of participants, primaries were statewide affairs in which broader swaths of the population tend to vote and otherwise involve themselves.

As such, putting in place an effective ground game was as important (if not more so) in New Hampshire as it was in Iowa.

The two events are a week apart: first the Iowa Caucus, then the New Hampshire Primary. And from certain political perspectives, the two states are as different as night and day. New Hampshire is traditionally more liberal, more industrial, more focused on industries such as Finance and High Tech. Perhaps more importantly — and as I learned during the campaign — much of the state from a political perspective can be viewed as a suburb of Boston.

But people are people, and I really enjoyed getting to know many of them in the Granite State. Early on in my efforts, I found a young man named Jim Demers, who, in 1982, had run for Congress and lost. We became great friends and he really helped me to navigate the state and educated me as to who the key players were and so on.

I also ran into Jeanne Shaheen, the State's current Senior Senator, who had run Carter's 1976 campaign.

Best of all (at least from my perspective), she was a Missouri native. I spent a lot of time picking her brain as to how best organize a campaign in New Hampshire.

Thus, my organization started to take shape. I enlisted Joyce Aboussie, my St. Louis campaign manager, whose father was a supporter of mine dating back to my run for City Council Board of Aldermen back in 1971. Joyce was a recent graduate from St. Louis University and a real hard worker, very smart, and an extraordinary political organizer and fundraiser. She had run my political operation in my Congressional District for ten years.

Her efforts were pivotal in helping me to get re-elected in a very competitive swing district. I asked her to set up shop for me in Iowa. As a result of all this activity — most of which took place in 1985 and 1986 — I became more and more convinced that if I was willing to take this plunge that I might have a chance to win the nomination.

But I didn't actually make the commitment formally until 1987. Among other attendees at my formal announcement was Missouri Senator Tom Eagleton, who is best remembered as having been selected as George McGovern's 1972 running mate only to be forced to withdraw abruptly in the wake of discoveries of his previously undisclosed bouts with depression. Also in attendance was Jack Buck, the longtime announcer for the St. Louis Cardinals. We held the event in the Grand Ballroom of Union Station in St. Louis. My whole family was there, and the room was packed with supporters.

I made a speech that I do not in retrospect believe was a very good one laying out my policies. Thankfully, I did have a lot of friends in the room, among them August Busch, III—Chairman of beverage company Anheuser-Busch. He held a big fundraiser for me the night of my announcement. We raised a fair amount of money that night, but the total tally for my entire campaign was $12 million, a drop in the bucket compared to the billion-dollar political cash engines of the present day. Presidential campaigns raise that sum in one day — day after day.

The year 1988 was before the era of PACs and super-PACs, but even then, it was a pathetically small sum, which nonetheless took great effort to acquire. And though I spent a lot of time calling on donors — large ones that had helped the likes of Walter Mondale, Jimmy Carter, and other Democrats in the past — fundraising was an exceedingly difficult task. Most of the bankroll came in units of $1,000 or less. And I was unable to devote sufficient time to the effort because I had to be on the ground in Iowa and New Hampshire.

I'd like to take this opportunity to describe a relationship that I developed as an illustration of the importance of personal interaction in even this most national of election processes.

The people in Iowa were consistent in advising me that if I was to stand any chance in their state, securing the support of Connie Clark, then Director of the American Federation of State, County, and Municipal Employees (AFSCME) in Cedar Rapids, was essential.

Cedar Rapids is the second largest city in Iowa, whose current population of approximately 132,000 ranks it in between Coral Springs, FL and Round Rock, TX in the low 200s of municipal citizen count. But it is a touchstone for the Iowa Caucuses, Iowa politics in general, and was thus the key to securing the Democratic nomination (and Presidency) for candidates ranging from Jimmy Carter to Barack Obama

It all illustrates the following observation by Stu Eizenstat, a former advisor to President Carter, reported in the Washington Post early in my campaign: "(running for the presidency in Iowa) is more at the level of running for county clerk." (Washington Post, March 29, 1987)

To win Cedar Rapids, I needed Connie's endorsement. So, I met her, courted her so to speak, and found that she was a wonderful person and highly regarded by everybody in the county and in the city. But meeting her once wouldn't cut it; so I spent a great deal of time getting to know her. She lived with her husband in a small house in Cedar Rapids, and we must have hit it off because she repeatedly invited me to stay at her house.

But this didn't mean she was endorsing my candidacy. She let me know early on that she was taking a close look at all the contestants and would inform me of her decision when it was appropriate to do so. Connie has been accused in the national and local press of being overly invested in the political courtship by aspiring presidents, but she took the process deeply to heart. As she told The Washington Post in 1987 "I'm really torn by this, it's not easy" (Same article).

Our interactions were long and extensive. She told me right away that she was impressed with me, wanted to talk to me, but that didn't mean she had made the decision to endorse me.

Meanwhile, she and her neighbors couldn't have been nicer. Dozens of regular folks would meet me at the airport in towns like Ottumwa and drive me all around their towns making introductions. They would put me up at their house; they would cook food; they were wonderful, and became wonderful friends. And they did it all for nothing. They were just volunteers.

They believed in our democracy. They believed in our form of government. They believed that they, as citizens, had a responsibility and a role in supporting candidates in whom they believed. They were living examples of the citizens' obligations required to retain our experiment in self government.

Connie had two huge German Shepherd dogs that she truly loved. During my visits, they would sit on the couch with me, covering the back of my serge-blue suit with dog hair. Connie would laugh and brush off my coat. Once, during the end of a stint in New Hampshire, and on my way back to Iowa from the Manchester (NH) airport, I spotted and picked up a couple of glass figurine German Shepherds as a gift for her. She was absolutely thrilled that I had enough regard for her to give her such a thoughtful present.

But she still hadn't made her decision. However, at that point, she'd at least narrowed her choice down to me and (future President) Joe Biden. She told me that she liked us both, but had to take into account that Biden was a Senator while I was (merely) a congressman.

I stayed on her, but she was truly torn. Finally, she called and invited me and my entire family to the big Cedar Rapids 4th of July celebration. It's an all-day event featuring a picnic lunch and picnic dinner.

She also invited us to stay at her house. Then she hung up.

I couldn't help hoping that this was a good sign, but for all I knew, she was giving the same treatment to Biden; so I wasn't sure. We arrived, picnicked, and awaited the fireworks display. Just as the show began, she turned to me and said, "Dick, I made my decision. It was a hard decision. But I'm going to be for you."

I really felt this to be the culmination of all the work we had done in Iowa. It wasn't decisive (it takes, after all, more than a single endorsement to win the Iowa Caucuses), but it certainly was important. So, we just kept working and working. One of my strongest assets was my mother Loreen, who was eighty years old at the time, and moved to the State for six months. Whether I was there or not, she would give her own stump speech. She was a great (if biased) verifier of my character and background. We modeled her role upon what Jimmy Carter's mother Lillian had done in 1976.

It was a big night, again the culmination of months and years of work by many people. Illinois Senator Paul Simon came in second, followed by the party's ultimate nominee, Massachusetts Governor Michael Dukakis.

Several months earlier, Joe Biden had withdrawn his name primarily due to a widely reported issue of plagiarism — a sequence of events, which, in today's political environment would be considered laughable (he would not have been forced to withdraw over this).

When I was introduced at a downtown Des Moines hotel to the theme from Rocky, I said, "We've won the first battle, but the struggle does not end here. It's only just begun. I ask for your help not just to win an election. I ask for your help to change America and give it back its soul." (LA Times: 2/9/88).

It is important to add here that the Iowa victory would not have happened without the incredible work of my entire family and thousands of volunteers from Iowa, Missouri and many other states. Also very important was the work of 80 Members of Congress — many of whom made repeated trips to Iowa to campaign for me.

And special credit must go to Joyce Aboussie, who lived in Iowa for a year and really managed the entire Iowa effort. For 40 years she was like a member of our family and was really responsible for allowing me to render public service over those years.

Without all of the people mentioned here — standing beside me and helping me — I could have done nothing.

Throughout my life I experienced a simple truth: one person alone can achieve very little but people working together can achieve anything. The magic that occurs from working together comes from the fact that people sacrifice their own selfish interests for the success of the group. In other words they love one another.

It really is the human story. Unlike pre-humans we evolved to have a bigger brain and invented language to be able to communicate complex thoughts and ideas. All of that allowed humans to dominate our planet over many larger physically superior creatures.

The secret sauce is WORKING TOGETHER and democracy is the highest expression of that.

It was a big night, again the culmination of months of shoe leather work. By my count, I spent over three hundred days and nights in Iowa, and about half as many in New Hampshire. All the while, I was still a member of Congress and remained the Chairman of the Democratic Caucus. The business of national legislation had to continue — my higher political ambitions notwithstanding. And, while I had important work to do in Washington, I was also obliged to return to my district in St. Louis on at least a few occasions to listen to and deal with my constituents.

I chose not to resign from Congress to pursue the Presidency. This is a decision that every candidate who holds office must face, and there are merits to both sides of the argument. But I chose to retain my seat, at least through the primaries, thinking that if I won the nomination, I would probably yield my seat because I could not contemporaneously run for both President and Congress in the General Election.

In addition to all the above, I was also compelled to visit other jurisdictions beyond Iowa and New Hampshire. My role as Caucus Chair brought me routinely to the South, a region that also was essential to any prospects I was entertaining of winning the nomination or the Presidency. My belief was always that if you were going to win a general election as a Democrat, you had to have support in the South and you needed backing from more conservative and moderate Democrats. You couldn't run as a liberal. You couldn't run on a left wing set of proposals.

Our efforts to secure support within the Democratic Caucus yielded over eighty members who formally endorsed my candidacy. All of them spent a lot of time on the ground for me — not only in Iowa and New Hampshire — but also their own state.

Again, we had one week between Iowa and New Hampshire. So, on the night of our Iowa victory, we had to board a private plane to fly from Des Moines to Manchester with ice and snow on the ground in both places. We had a hairy landing in Manchester, and when I got there I knew I was up against a real tough foe — Massachusetts Governor Michael Dukakis. As I mentioned earlier, from a political perspective, much of the state of New Hampshire is a suburb of Boston. As such, I was pretty sure I couldn't win the state, but I really needed to come in second in order to stay in the race. Paul Simon had mounted a really good campaign in New Hampshire and worked furiously in the state as the voting day approached.

In the end, while Dukakis won with 36 percent of the vote, we were able to eke out second place with 20 percent, edging out Simon's 17 percent. My aides in the state convinced me, on primary day, to spend the entire day calling voters and trying to convince them to vote for me. That effort may very well have given me the edge over Simon.

At any rate, my second-place finish allowed me to remain in the race. Had I placed any lower, likely I would have been compelled to withdraw that night.

So, after that major achievement, it was on to South Dakota, whose primary took place the following week. Fortunately, I had the support of the state's only Congressman, Tom Daschle, who also in 1988 successfully ran for Senate and went on to become Minority Leader of the Upper Chamber. Tom was a good friend of mine and campaigned hard for me in his state. We did run a TV ad against Dukakis in which we made light of a comment by the Governor that suggested that endive was a major agricultural product for the United States. Obviously, such a comment showed him to be out of step with voters in the region.

Lo and behold, we had a big victory in South Dakota. And the next step was — in contrast to the current day — a slimmed down version of Super Tuesday. In 2020, the day featured fourteen state primaries along with a caucus in American Samoa. But in 1988, the number of participating Super Tuesday states was ten and featured a good portion of the Midwest including my home state of Missouri.

According to my pollster, after the South Dakota win, I was far and away ahead in the polls in all of those ten Super Tuesday states. At the time, he was convinced that I would be the nominee and urged me to start thinking about the General Election. This was not what I wanted to hear at the time, and I told him we needed to keep our focus on the ten races immediately before us.

The big problem then was money. To be blunt, I had none left — none even to hire staff, buy TV advertising, rent cars, or finance other campaign essentials. I'd spent it all in the first three states. I was reduced to running alone around ten states as best I could to try to put together the votes. My opponents were not similarly constrained. I clearly remember walking into a hotel room in Dallas on a Thursday night, seeing the ads that were being run in our primary, and lamenting the reality that we had none.

Dukakis, for instance, ran an ad saying that I had flip-flopped on Medicare and Abortion. Al Gore did the same thing. Meanwhile, as my opponents were running negative ads, I wasn't running ads of any kind. This really worried me, but all I could do was try to hang on through the Tuesday voting cycle.

That Sunday, I was in the Rio Grande Valley in South Texas where there were a lot of Hispanic constituents. I was about to do a press conference with the sheriff of a particular county. Before I'd even gotten out of bed in the motel, my pollster called me again and said, "Dick, I have to amend my statement of last Wednesday. You're now behind in all the Super Tuesday states except Missouri. I don't think you're going to be the nominee."

Well, that did not make for a pleasant press conference for me; but sure enough, on Election Day 1988 I lost all the Super Tuesday states, mainly to Dukakis and Gore.

Strike that—I did win Missouri—good old Missouri!

But while that was really the practical end of my campaign, we decided to press on. I thought maybe we could put things back together in the next state, Michigan. I had huge support from the United Auto Workers Union, which of course was and is a critical voting bloc in that state.

So we went straight to Michigan and worked there for a week or two. I thought I had a good chance, since I also had the support of Frank Kelley, the state's longtime Attorney General, who holds the record for the longest continuous tenure in any state for that office in American history.

What I didn't know was that they had very few polling places in Michigan — perhaps thirteen across the entire state. I also underestimated African American participation concentrated near many of the polling stations, all at a time when Jesse Jackson was mounting a strong campaign of his own. Michigan is a caucus state, and when the results came in, Jackson had won more than half of the votes and I finished well behind this tally.

This put the final nail in the coffin of the Gephardt 1988 campaign. I turned my attention back to Congress, withdrew in time to refile for my seat, and, ultimately, to win re-election.

In terms of my 1988 presidential run, I view it as a very positive experience. I have no regrets or recriminations to report. There were a lot of reasons we didn't ultimately succeed, but—like so much in life—the learning experience was invaluable (and unattainable in any other way). I came out of it with a sense of the entire country. I understood, so much better than I ever had, the diversity of the America, the economic and cultural similarities, and differences which both unite and divide us.

To put the matter in perspective, the United States is the equivalent, in terms of population and diversity, of twenty European countries. Running for President brought these realities to me in clear focus.

Not everybody wants to do this, but it was an invaluable, rewarding experience, in no small measure because of all the wonderful people I met. These days, people ask me for my views for the future of America. And I always say I'm positive because of the American people, the vast majority of whom are really good souls.

Nobody's perfect, nobody avoids mistakes, nobody avoids wrongdoing. But the vast majority of the American people are of true quality are centered on the right values. They love their country. They care about their family. They care about their community. They care about their state. It really doesn't get better than that, and I believe that's the reason we've had such a vibrant democracy for all these years.

And as for the 1988 Presidential Election, history tells us of the outcome. Dukakis won the Democratic nomination and entered the General Election with a sizeable margin over then-Vice President George H.W. Bush. Ultimately, Bush won—in no small part due to a series of negative campaign ads he ran against Governor Dukakis. He served a single term, followed by eight years of Bill Clinton, eight years of his son George W. Bush, two terms for Barack Obama, and a single term for Donald Trump who was succeeded by our current president, Joe Biden.

But my calling was back to Congress, to higher levels of leadership in that important legislative body.

It was a journey, unfolding in subsequent chapters, that marked the destiny of my life.

CHAPTER 6

Majority Leadership (with the Help of the Minority)

A s mentioned in the last chapter, after losing in the Michigan Democratic Primary and knowing my presidential hopes were not to be realized, I had another decision to make. I had to move quickly if I was to seek another term in Congress. A number of candidates had already filed for the Democratic nomination for my district, so there was no time to lose. In late March 1988, I traveled to the Missouri State Capital in Jefferson City and filed.

I didn't consider my re-election to be a foregone conclusion, but I had laid such a strong political foundation — in the district, in the state and frankly, the presidential race — that I knew I stood a good chance. Nonetheless, I had to work at it and went door to door just as I had done in previous races. Fortunately, we were able to win. The "on the ground" organization Joyce Aboussie had established in the district was as good as it gets.

After the victory, it was back to Congress where I was still a junior member. I began to ponder how to reestablish a position in the leadership and how I could be more effective in trying to get things done for my district and for the country.

The opportunity to do so came rather quickly, and in unantici-pated fashion. In June 1989, something extraordinary happened. Jim

Wright, who at that time was Speaker of the House (having taken over after Tip O'Neill retired), resigned from the Congress due to what then was considered a major ethics scandal. It was an episode that in today's political environment might not even merit news coverage. The charges against him stated that he published a series of books and sold a large number of them to major campaign donors—purportedly as a backdoor compensation and campaign finance scheme. Newt Gingrich, then something of a backbencher in the Republican Caucus, led the investigation.

Newt argued that this was a violation of Ethics Rules passed in 1977 (in the wake of a pay increase for Members from 47,000 to 57,000 per year) that strictly limited outside compensation for seat holders. At the outset, nobody believed the complaint had much substance. But the sequence took place at a time when the Democratic Caucus was placing a significant focus on reform. More than ten years after the fact, we were still trying to justify those pay increases from 1977.

The Ethics Committee traditionally took every matter brought to its attention very seriously, as they should have. However, in this case, they were truly wrestling with whether Wright had actually broken the rules, and, if so, what sort of penalty should be imposed. As they pondered these issues, so much pressure mounted that Wright ultimately chose to resign.

I have vivid memories of his tearful, farewell address, given on May 31, 1989, where he stated:

"When vilification becomes an accepted form of political debate, when negative campaigning becomes a full-time occupation, when members of each party become self-appointed vigilantes carrying out personal vendettas against members of the other party, in God's name that is not what this institution is about. . . All of us, in both political parties, must resolve to bring this mindless cannibalism to an end."

More than thirty years later, I believe we still have a lot of work to do.

But "comity" was a problem even back then. Wright was not just a typical Congressman. He enlisted in the Air Force right after Pearl Harbor and earned the Distinguished Flying Cross for his service in the Second World War. He served sixteen terms in the House of Representatives and rose to the position of Speaker of the House.

On the morning of November 22, 1963, as part of the last speech he would ever give, President Kennedy said this of him: "He speaks for Fort Worth and he speaks for the country, and I don't know any city that is better represented in the Congress of the United States than Fort Worth."

And then, within a blink of an eye, he was gone.

The hits kept coming that Spring. Contemporaneous to the Wright episode, Democratic California Congressman and House Majority Whip Tony Coelho found himself the target of an investigation for having accepted funding from a Savings and Loan enterprise (at a time when Savings and Loan institutions were in the midst of a huge scandal themselves — one which ultimately required a multi-billion-dollar taxpayer bailout) — and used the proceeds to purchase Non-Investment Grade (Junk) Bonds. The optics were less than ideal, suggesting that Coelho had received special treatment from a scandal-plagued industry. But he was never charged with criminal activity.

Nonetheless, he was forced to resign as well. Tony was probably my closest friend in my time in the House. He was a strong supporter in my 1988 run for the Presidential nomination. This was a crushing blow to all of us in Congress.

So, lo and behold, and just six short months after the 1988 election, the two top positions in the Democratic Congressional Caucus became available. Tom Foley, Member for the 5th District in the State of Washington, ascended to the Speaker's spot, leaving the second slot in the hierarchy — House Majority Leader — up for grabs. Considering the support that I had received from members in the 1988 Presidential Election, in addition to my experience as Leader of the Democratic Congressional Caucus, I believed that I stood a good chance to win the position.

As a first step, I brought in for assistance a gentleman named Tom O'Donnell, who had run the Democratic Congressional Campaign Committee under Tony Coelho.

He became (and remained for many years) my Chief of Staff, and friend, and set about to organize my campaign for Majority Leader. It was a tough slog. I had a number of opponents who were very adept at running within the caucus, including a couple of highly skilled and experienced members from the (critical) South.

But we pulled it out, and incredibly, during the month of July 1989, I became Majority Leader.

My main objective was to bring about discipline to the Democratic House Majority, and my first test was to attempt to add efficiency to the Budget Act and Appropriations Cycle. Immediately after assuming my post, I said to my staff, "We have to get the budget done on time (which would be in the spring of the next year). And this means that we have to get all of the appropriation bills done right after that in the summer of 1990."

Meeting the deadline was something that had never been done before, and there were many skeptics quick to remind us that there are thirteen separate appropriation bills brought out by Subcommittees of the Appropriations Committee. It involved countless meetings with the Chairs and Ranking Members of these groups.

Somehow, through all this hard work (and featuring a great deal of compromise), we were able to complete the Appropriations Cycle on time. I was very proud of that achievement. I've always felt that if Congress were going to operate effectively, it had to do its work in a timely fashion. With this ethic driving us, we also completed the 1990 budget bill by its stated deadline.

But then, in August of 1990, another extraordinary event happened, and it served to disrupt all our plans. Saddam Hussein and the Iraqi Military invaded and captured Kuwait — a nation that was a great ally and major exporter of energy to the United States. Quite appropriately, President Bush treated this as an emergency situation, and his first step was to form an alliance of countries around the world to repel that invasion and protect the sovereignty of Kuwait.

At the same time, Congressional leaders began a series of meetings with the President to determine the appropriate response. Early in those conversations, President Bush indicated his belief that he had the unilateral authority to deal with this in the Executive Branch and did not need Congressional approval to respond militarily. We knew at the time that he was in part motivated by a fear that he lacked the votes in Congress to authorize military action.

My colleagues and I disagreed with his position. Speaker Foley, and Senate Majority Leader George Mitchell (D, ME) and I told him, "You have to have a vote. You may not win it. We don't know whether you will win it. We're not going to take a position one way or another on it. The members have to decide it themselves. But you have to have a vote if you're going to take a democracy to war. The people have to have a vote on that. You can't just do it as an executive."

Eventually and reluctantly, he agreed. The House and Senate then entered into a huge debate over the War Resolution of 1990. My message to my caucus was this, "Everybody has to decide this on their own." I informed them that I would vote "NO" and stated the reasons for my position. I said, "I just I do not think we can settle disputes all over the world, even though they may be worthy disputes. Even though Saddam Hussein may be a really bad guy and doing horrible things, I don't see why we should spill American blood to save this tiny Emirate, this tiny country in the Middle East, from another monster in the Middle East who just wanted all the money."

In my mind, the decision to declare war is the most important responsibility assumed by elected officials. In order take such a decision, you must use care and understanding to determine your best estimates as to death and injury of your own troops, enemy troops, and civilian populations. You must understand the costs also not only in blood but also in treasure.

I compared the situation to our entry into the Second World War, where the choice was both obvious and imperative. In addition, I was mindful of the reality that a nation at war, even if victorious, consigns itself to remain in the area of conflict for years or perhaps decades. America, for instance, retains troops in Germany and Japan three generations after defeating them in the Second World War. And, for what it's worth, we have been compelled to maintain military and other forms of support for Iraq more than thirty years after the conclusion of Gulf War I (to say nothing of the reality that we felt compelled, more than a decade after this war, to attack Iraq and Hussein a second time).

I did not take my choice to vote against Gulf War I lightly, and, as subsequent history demonstrates, it ran against Congressional consensus. The House and Senate approved the war resolution, and off our troops went.

Fortunately, we repelled Saddam Hussein's army very quickly, and drove them back to Baghdad in a short period with minimal loss of life to U.S. forces. It was also very helpful that George H.W. Bush had put together a United Nations and world coalition of nations to stand with us in this struggle. Perhaps as importantly (and wisely in my judgment), Bush decided to limit our actions to the objectives he had articulated at the outset: to remove the Iraqi presence in Kuwait. He resisted the temptation to enter Iraq, remake the country, and remove Saddam Hussein. Once we had repelled the invaders and had driven them back to their own country (which we did in a short period) he did not want to stay there. He pulled our troops out. We stopped everything.

And that was a very, very wise decision on his part. This war did not go on and on forever.

Again, this was a lesson we probably should have retained for our later incursions into Iraq and Afghanistan, a topic that I will cover in subsequent chapters.

Immediately after Gulf War ended, the President asked me and House Minority Leader and Illinois Republican Bob Michel to lead a delegation of House members (Democrats and Republicans) to travel to the region and assess the carnage. We left Andrews Air Force Base on August 31, 1990, and when we arrived in Kuwait, what we found was truly shocking. The environmental damage wrought by Hussein was beyond horrifying —much of it clearly undertaken at the point of their retreat to wreak as much permanent damage on the way out as was possible.

Having never visited Kuwait, I was unaware that the oil in that country was positioned relatively close to the ground. When we arrived, we observed flaming oil wells and actual lakes of oil on fire virtually everywhere we looked. The location of crude being at the very upper range of the geo-topography meant that it took little more than a lit match to ignite a raging inferno.

So, when we entered our Kuwait City, escorted by our military, it was like entering hell. There was fire everywhere you looked — smoke and thick oil. To breath properly and keep the oil out of your lungs, it was necessary to wear facial coverings (sound familiar?). We visited the remaining troops, and, almost to a person, they were begging for our assistance to send them home. Many of them came up to me and said, "You've got to get us out of here — we're all going to die of oil poisoning. Our lungs are full of oil. Our nose is full of oil. This is a hellish disaster." Of course, this made us want to work harder to get our people out as fast as we could.

I can conclude from this experience that Saddam Hussein was a certified demon, as no other description would suit what I observed in terms of the human and environmental damage he was responsible for in Kuwait. Ultimately, the irascible Red Adair — the famous independent daredevil — stepped in and got the fires under control. Our troops came home, and Kuwait was placed in a position where it was able to put itself back together as a nation.

Immediately thereafter, our delegation was asked to come to Saudi Arabia to meet the King and to accept the Royal Family's thanks for our efforts. The Saudis were particularly appreciative because they lived with the significant and justifiable fear that, had Hussein prevailed in Kuwait, he might very well turn his hostile attention to Riyadh. My belief is that President Bush did little to discourage—and may have in fact, encouraged — this trepidation as a means of solidifying Saudi support for our military initiative.

I had not been to Riyadh since my above-described visit in the lead-up to the Soviet and Afghan war in the late 1970s. A great deal had changed and evolved during the intervening years, and it was noticeable immediately upon our arrival.

It was like entering Rome in its empire days. Every avenue featured a roundabout with a glorious piece of sculpture in the center. When we arrived at the King's palace, he insisted that the entire twenty-five-member delegation stay there as his personal guests. We were then escorted into more than two dozen luxury, multi-room suites, with grand pianos, upscale artwork, and other similar amenities.

It was about 2:30 a.m. when we entered the palace, whereupon an enormous buffet feast awaited us. I'll just say that the food was incredible, but it was impossible not to mark the stark contrast to the suffering we had observed in Kuwait.

And that was that.

Upon our return, it was time to revert to the (by contrast, more mundane) work on budgetary matters. As was perhaps inevitable, budget considerations had stalled during the Middle East crisis, and all parties were eager to put it back on track. More than this, leadership on all sides were committed to reversing the trajectory, begun during the Reagan years, of larger deficits every year. Reagan had initiated a series of large tax cuts without due consideration of offsetting spending reductions. All parties agreed that — though the numbers entirely pale in comparison to today's gargantuan deficits — those that were accumulating at the time presented a huge financial challenge to the United States. We all realized that difficult as it might be, we needed to work together to solve this problem.

I should emphasize we were not simply looking at deficit shortfalls for the period in question. Everyone could see that the problem, if not proactively addressed, would grow into perpetuity. We met many times with President Bush on the topic in those early days, and each time either Tom Foley, George Mitchell, or I would say to the president, "We're happy to do this, we agree with you, it needs to be done. We want to work with you in doing this. But our only question is whether everything on the table? In other words, are we going to consider both spending cuts, which you have to, or can we include in that menu of things to do tax increases? We're not saying we're going to come to that conclusion, but we think everything has to be on the table so that we have all the options."

He immediately replied that he could not put a tax hike on the table because he had given his word that he would not raise taxes. Specifically (and famously), during his acceptance speech in the 1988 Republican National convention, he uttered the following phrase: "Read my lips. No new taxes." He told us that if he went back on this pledge, he'd be crucified.

"We understand, we know that's what you said, and we understand your feeling about this," we replied, "but we do not want to participate in a budget summit where everything is not on the table. We're not saying we're going to raise taxes. We don't know that that will be a conclusion of this negotiation. But we just think all the options have to be on the table to be fair, honest, and to be able to come to an agreement that we can try to get through Congress."

After multiple meetings, not only did we fail to reach an agreement on terms, we didn't even have a framework for holding a budget summit. The President invited the leaders from both parties to dinner at the White House as a way to possibly break the impasse. At some point he said, "OK. I get it. I think we need to do this summit. I'm willing to put everything on the table." George Mitchell happily complied, but with the following caveat: he asked for a letter from the President confirming that the summit would contemplate all deficit mitigation options, including tax increases.

Bush's shoulders visibly drooped at this suggestion. But then he looked up and said: "OK, I'll do it."

He called in Press Secretary Marlin Fitzwater and asked him to put out a statement to that effect, saying, "I'm going to write a letter to these folks and I'm going to tell them that we've agreed to have a budget summit. And that everything's going to be on the table, including taxes."

Fitzwater left the room with that instruction in hand and put out that press release that night. After dinner, while waiting outside for our cars to arrive, I found myself standing next to President Bush, who was nervously shifting back and forth, foot to foot. I could see his consternation, and I asked him what was wrong.

His reply was, "The fat is in the fire." I knew what he meant, and I empathized. I had experienced the negative impacts of "taking back my word," by retracting a promise to Tip O'Neill. But as formidable as Tip was, it was nothing compared to reversing course on an entire party and nation. Bush faced instantaneous rebukes from both sources. It may have been worse, in fact, from a party affiliation standpoint, owing to the long-standing Republican objective to minimize taxes.

Throughout the remainder of my career and my life, this story resonated with me, as well as taught an important lesson. Specifically, I believe that true, effective leadership requires compromise, and it is especially difficult when such compromise requires confrontation with strong opposition from one's own side. George H. W. Bush was a real leader. He was someone who held strongly his own convictions. But he also understood that to govern this huge, diverse country — to move this group of five hundred and thirty-five people that we call Congress to make difficult decisions — it was necessary to take stands that were unpopular within his own party.

With Bush's promissory letter in hand, we began to work on the budget deal in earnest. It was an enormous challenge. Early on, we decided to convene all the chairs of all the pertinent committees and subcommittees, as well as their ranking members in the minority. We all felt that this was the only way to proceed, particularly because the committee leaders were the true subject matter experts on many budgetary matters. But negotiating across party lines with such a large group of participants — often all in the same room at the same time — was a huge task.

How do you get all these people to work together and listen to one another? We decided to task each Congressional Committee (House and Senate) to work in a bipartisan fashion to produce the cuts needed in their area of jurisdiction to meet their overall goals. But ultimately, we had to reconvene the larger group in order to compile a coherent overall package. It was an enormously complicated mission. Tom Foley asked me to lead our side while George Mitchell commanded the Senate contingent in cooperation with Senate Minority Leader Bob Dole and House Minority Leader Bob Michel.

The four of us worked day in and day out on this compromise. The heavy lifting transpired in June of 1990, and we established a self-imposed deadline of late October or early November, primarily because we did not want to extend the talks past the mid-term election, which would usher in a new Congress.

Sometime in October, it became obvious that these negotiations were leaking into the press and the public. And the one thing you know is that if you're trying to negotiate a very complicated matter, you can't do it in public. We had to control — in fact, to the greatest extent possible, eliminate — rumors and questions as to the specific program cuts and tax increases we were contemplating. Public comment would force members to take premature positions, often inaccurately reported. For example, the press would report rumors about, say, a gas tax, which would force members to either come out definitively against it or risk political Armageddon.

We knew that for the negotiations to have any chance to succeed, we would have to leave the Capitol and move to a private location protected from the din. We selected Andrews Air Force Base, in suburban Maryland, approximately ten miles outside the Washington city limit. There's an Officers Club on the base, with dining, overnight accommodations, and, most importantly, the privacy and security of a military installation. Thus, off to Andrews we went. The entire bipartisan Congressional Budget Group, along with Bush representatives — most notably Dick Darman, the Director of the Office of Management and Budget and a gentleman who is thought to have been a big influence in Bush's reversal on the "read my lips" pledge, and John Sununu, a Cuban-born former Governor of New Hampshire who was serving as White House Chief of Staff. Together, we were there to represent President Bush in the negotiations.

What I remember from the Caucus was endless meetings and a lot of hot fudge sundaes, Bob Dole's favorite food. I loved Bob Dole, a true American hero — a patriot — who cared about the country first and foremost. He was a strong conservative, but he always placed the country over party.

Slowly, but surely, we began to put the pieces together for a deal. By that time, Newt Gingrich had risen to the role of Minority Whip. I vividly remember his presence, but also the fact that throughout the negotiation, he neither spoke nor even paid attention, preferring instead to pass the hours reading magazines. One time I said to him, "Why aren't you working on this?" And he responded by saying, "I'm not going to be for this. It is a politically unpopular package. It's going to cut spending. It's going to raise some taxes. I will oppose."

I went back to Darman and said, "Dick, I think you got a problem here because the whip on the Republican side of the House is not going to be for this." And Darman said to me, "Oh, don't worry, we have talked to him. He is going to be for this." I said, "Okay, but I just needed you to hear what I heard."

Painstakingly, we put this whole package together and brought it out on the floor. Before we put the final pieces in place, Darman and I went back to President Bush, and I said, "If I'm going to produce half my members to vote for this, and the Republicans are going to produce half their members, I really would like you to consider cutting defense a little bit more. It doesn't have to be a huge cut. But I've got to get the vote of some liberals who are going to hate these spending cuts in domestic programs. And if I can point to a little bit of a cut more in defense, it will help me pick up some needed votes." We had been negotiating day and night without sleep. I had talked to the President and Darman before we were to wrap it all up. I really needed Darman's push, and I'll never forget standing in my office when Darman called me back to let me know that the President could not sign off on the additional defense cuts. He threw the ball back in my court, told me it was up to me, and asked me what I was going to do.

I went back to Tom Foley, and I told him what had happened and said, "I don't know if we can get the votes, but this is where we are and we got to make this compromise. I don't think we can back up now. We've done too much. We have gone too far." Foley agreed with me. I called Darman back and said, "Okay, we'll try. We're going to do our best."

We went out on the floor, and we argued the case for another three days and nights. And when the vote was taken, we lost. I was able to produce half of my members, but the Republicans could not match in no small measure because of Gingrich holding press conferences saying that no Republicans should vote for this budget. And privately, Newt told me, "Look, I'm trying to win the House back and I can't win the House back if we vote for this mess." As such, the Republicans had failed to delivery their share of the needed votes.

After the budget resolution failed, we were really at sea. It was late November/early December after the 1990 mid-term elections. I went back to Darman, and he was as flummoxed as I, saying "What are we going to do?" I replied "There's only one thing I think could work. I have got to pick up more than half of my members to make up for the Republican members that will not vote for this. So, you have to give me that cut in defense that I talked to you and the President about a few days ago."

He went back to President Bush, who agreed to that cut. This led to another vote, which was successful by a small margin. It was largely due to the addition of several of the more liberal members of the Democratic Caucus who were swayed by the additional defense cuts. Nobody ever wants to vote for a budget deficit reduction package because it only leads to political pain (the payoff, in the form of a better fiscal financial picture, comes later). A "yes" vote requires endorsing reductions in popular programs or always unpopular tax increases. And, when you reach the end of a project such as this one, it always risks blowing up because it is so hard to convince that committee of 535 people called Congress to do things that are really difficult.

I remember after it passed everybody immediately went home, leaving only myself and one Republican member on the floor. After we adjourned, I walked out to the speaker's lobby, which was right off the House chamber, and there was Dick Darman.

We didn't say a word. We hugged one another. We both understood how difficult this had been — how close we had come to failure. I was grateful to him for all the hard work and effort he had put forward. I had admired him for the honesty and forthrightness that he showed through the entire process. We had built trust between one another. And in the end, that is what is needed in any organization of human beings that is trying to accomplish difficult tasks. I always remember

how I grieved the day he died — at the too-young age of sixty-four -—
after a long battle with leukemia.

I considered him and George H.W. Bush to be true patriots —
wonderful Americans who always tried to do the right thing for the
country, whether or not it was the right thing for their party or themselves. They were always willing to put country over party or self.

I truly believe that this work put us on the track for those years of
budget surplus that emerged in the late 1990s. Federal outlays declined
across the decade, while revenues climbed for most of the period.

By 1998 and through 2001, the country actually enjoyed a budget
surplus, and I believe that our 1990 budget bill was an essential contributor. It was the first necessary step to getting control of the Federal
financial situation. It featured spending cuts and modest (mostly opti-
cal) tax increases. But for the first time ever, we had created hard caps
for discretionary spending, along with the concept of "pay as you go"
— an ideal model for the management of public finance.

That model began blowing up in the early part of the new century
and, of course, has been completely obliterated in recent years. But
it was that originally failed process that led to this summit and this
innovation of creating caps on discretionary spending. Dick Darman
always said the most important thing we did in this bill was to get these
discretionary caps.

At any rate, it got us on the road to a balanced budget, if only for
a brief interval. Today, we have the Modern Monetary Theory, which
for the most part posits that government should simply spend all it
desires and finance it by printing money. Inflation is the only consideration that should constrain spending according to MMT advocates.
I do not believe that is true in the real world, and we certainly did
not believe it during the period described in this chapter. Instead, we
tried to operate the public budget like a family or company budget.

However we understood the Federal budget should run a deficit during economic recessions but not during good economic times. During these times anything that required spending had to be paid for in identifiable, straightforward ways that did not disrupt the prospects for future prosperity or incite crippling inflation.

These were the highlights as I recall them from my early days as House Majority Leader. We faced a number of difficult challenges and encountered many surprises along the way. Throughout, one message resonated: our best efforts came through compromise that catalyzed consensus.

To this day, I believe it is the only way for our country and democracy to succeed.

With John Kerry (right)

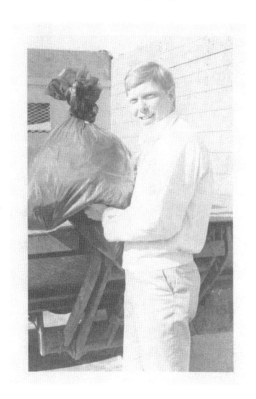

Another one of many workdays as a trash collector in the 1990's

Meeting with President Jimmy Carter (left)

Meeting with President of Russia Boris Yeltsin (left)

Meeting with President George W. Bush (left) in my office

Meeting students in congressional district

Meeting with General Schwarzkopf (second
from left) and members of congress

Meeting with Prime Minister of Israel Ehud Barak (center)

One of many workdays being a trash collector in the 1990's

Meeting with Senator Ted Kennedy (center) and
his son Patrick Kennedy (right)

Meeting with Secretary of State Colin Powell (second from left) and members of congress Nancy Pelosi (right) and David Obey (second from right)

Meeting with Santa Claus at age 5

Shaking hands with President George H.W. Bush (left)

On Capital steps with other leaders (second left to right):
Dennis Hastert, Dick Armey, Tom Daschle, Trent Lott

Marching in a district parade during the 1990's

Meeting President George H.W. Bush (right) with Speaker Tom Foley (center)

Meeting President of South Africa Nelson Mandela (left)

Meeting with Margaret Thatcher (left)

Meeting with President George W. Bush (right), Tom
Daschle (second from left) and Trent Lott (left)

On a porch – one of many doors over 30 years

Meeting with Pope John Paul II (center) and President Bill Clinton (right)

Meeting with police officials in congressional district

Meeting with King Abdulla II of Jordan (left)

Meeting President Gorbachev of the Soviet Union (left) and President
George H. W. Bush (center) with my wife, Jane Gephardt (to my right).

Town hall meeting in district

CHAPTER 7

"The Beauty of Taking One for the Team"

I believe that the experiences described in the last chapter enabled me to gain a strong footing in my role as House Majority Leader, and I would like to take this opportunity to describe a couple of other legislative experiences that I had in the early '90s. I believe they embody both the challenges and the best modes of operation within an organization like the U.S. Congress.

I was deeply intent on being the best House Leader that I could be. An important aspect of this was scheduling grueling but essential processes such as budget and appropriations bills.

In 1991, I held to a strict itinerary for subcommittees and their members and told them that we had to get all that work done quickly, efficiently, and on time. The budget had to be completed by May 15, and then the appropriation bills would follow. Due to reasons somewhat out of our control (the first Gulf War), we missed some deadlines in 1990. I was determined that this wouldn't happen in 1991—and it didn't.

At the time, I was still under the full effects of the presidential bug that bit me in '88. Those around me sensed what I was feeling and encouraged me to consider another run in '92. They were sufficiently impressed with my efforts in the previous cycle that they believed it was worth another shot. At the time, the principal obstacle (in my mind and that of others) was the then enduring popularity of incumbent George H.W. Bush. My advisors acknowledged this but reminded me that in presidential politics (as in other life events) you never know what's going to happen.

They went on to argue that I was never going to be more popular than I was at that time in the critical early primary states of Iowa and New Hampshire. They reminded me of all the work I had put in, and all the relationships I had built in those two states and indeed across the country. The core of their message to me was that if I was going to run again — even think of running again — this was the time to do it. I had a national political brand and was House Majority Leader.

At the end of the day, I decided to bag it and chose instead to concentrate on the opportunity I had been given to be a leader in Congress. Again, the "political experts" of the day believed that the President's re-election was virtually inevitable. At that moment, his popularity — in large part because of his success with respect to Gulf War 1 — was at its peak. Nobody on the Democratic side was particularly eager to take him on.

That is until the young, brash, Governor of Arkansas stepped up. At first, the political establishment considered Bill Clinton's candidacy something of a side story — no one believed he had a chance to win. Even at the time, he was facing high profile criticisms of his relations with certain women, as well as investigations into his private business dealings while governor. But he pressed ahead, even after a disappointing showing in Iowa where he won only 2.8 percent of the caucus vote (the state gave an overwhelming majority to their favorite son and Vietnam fighter pilot Senator Tom Harkin).

Clinton, the Comeback Kid, also failed to win the next two primaries — New Hampshire and Maine — and won only Georgia out of the seven contests that held its primary on March 3rd. His big breakout came on March 10th, Super Tuesday, where he won eight out of eleven of the states in that cycle, including — critically — Florida, Texas, and my own state of Missouri.

By the time the July Convention in New York City came around, he was the unambiguous, consensus winner of the nomination. It was on to the General Election, which, as is widely known, took an odd turn with the entry of Texas oil man H. Ross Perot who ran as a thirdparty candidate.

His was a peculiar candidate in a strange election cycle. Perot actually quit the race at one point during the summer, but re-emerged in October to ultimately garner nearly 20 percent of the popular vote (though no electoral votes)—the best showing for an independent candidate since Former President Theodore Roosevelt ran under the Bull Moose banner in 1912. He collected 27 percent of the vote count and obstructed the path to re-election for his friend William Howard Taft, his former Secretary of War, culminating in the election of Woodrow Wilson.

Similarly, history makes a strong (though necessarily speculative) case that Perot's presence cost Bush the 1992 election and paved the path to victory for Clinton, who was elected despite winning only 43 percent of the popular vote. Had Perot not been on the ballot, would enough of those votes have gone to Bush to secure his re-election? We'll never know for sure.

My take is that irrespective of these other factors, Clinton ran a better campaign than Bush. He and his running mate (Al Gore, himself a multi-cycle and formidable presidential office seeker who actually won the popular vote against Clinton successor George W. Bush in 2000) showed great energy throughout. They toured the country endlessly. They were great communicators, great listeners, and showed empathy.

By contrast, George H.W. Bush and his running mate (his often-derided Vice President Dan Quayle), seemed detached, remote, and unsympathetic.

One (perhaps misreported) anecdote from the campaign illustrates the point. During a February campaign visit to the National Grocers Association in Florida, Bush seemed utterly bewildered by grocery bar code scanning technology—the fact that it had been ubiquitous in supermarkets for more than a decade notwithstanding. By contrast, Clinton positioned himself ideally as a man of the people, for example, responding to a heckling New York AIDs activist with the famous phrase, "I feel your pain."

The Good Ole Arkansas Boy vs. the New England Brahmin — both playing their roles to perfection. Bush never stood a chance.

Bush, of course, was not helped by the reality that a modest recession was transpiring during the campaign. Economic issues were re-emerging into the forefront of the minds of the electorate as the drama of the Middle East conflict began to fade. On a related note, I also believe that this led to the formation of the Democratic Leadership Council (DLC — created with the leadership of Al From, a former staffer of Representative Gillis Long). The DLC was a group of Democratic representatives, senators, and governors who came together because we all felt that the party had drifted a bit too far to the left.

The watchword for the group was moderation; its mission was to find a middle ground both ideologically and a politically. We felt that we were losing too many elections to candidates such as Ronald Reagan and George Bush because we had yielded the moderates to the Republicans. It was an interesting group, which included Senator Sam Nunn (Democrat, Georgia) and former Governor and son-in-law to Lyndon B. Johnson, Chuck Robb (Democrat, Virginia).

It also counted Bill Clinton among its members.

The DLC identified and built platforms that featured hope, opportunity, and the chance for all citizens to build a better life.

It was not a hugely successful effort, but it did change many people's perceptions of what the Democratic Party's ideals. It made it a more moderate, centrist party. And I think it did help Bill Clinton's election effort in 1992.

Immediately after the election, President-Elect Clinton invited George Mitchell (Democratic Leader in the Senate), Tom Foley (Speaker of the House), and me (House Majority Leader) to his home in Little Rock, Arkansas, to discuss the policy agenda for 102nd Congress. As you can probably imagine, Hillary took an active part in the conversation. Of course, she was at the time very interested in leading an effort on Health Care Reform.

When it was my turn to speak, I said, "Mr. President, I think the most important thing we have to do at the outset is to finish the job of balancing the budget." I then recounted all the difficulty and problems we had in getting the 1990 Bush Budget Summit budget done. I said, "We made a lot of progress, but we still have a looming big deficit, and my belief is that the only way he could get the economy to really go again and be strong again would be if we balance the budget. It would send the right signal to the financial markets. It would send the right signal to business people, particularly the owners of small companies."

His immediately reply was, "I think you're right. I watched what you all did. And I think it was important. And probably that's where we ought to start." I don't think Hillary was too pleased with that. But indeed, immediately after the inauguration we started to work on that 1993 budget bill. We used the same procedures we had deployed in 1990, engaging with all the individual Committee Chairs and Ranking Members, and involved all the individual members on committees. But this time we had the advantage of direct engagement on the part of the President and Vice President. In addition, we received enormous assistance from the administration's Director of the Office of Management and Budget, Leon Panetta, who went on to become Clinton's Chief of Staff. Later, he served under Obama as Director of Intelligence and then as Secretary of Defense.

In 1990, Leon was a congressman who had in fact been our Budget Chair during the 1990 episode.

We had a great experienced team that knew what it took to get the job done. But we had no illusions that that balancing the budget would be easy, particularly from a political perspective. Nonetheless, we all felt that we had to extend the momentum initiated in the 1990 Budget Summit and were highly determined to press ahead to the objective.

But, perhaps unsurprisingly, one of our biggest problems was Newt, whose power, influence, and visibility were all rising on the Republican side of the aisle. One day, he approached me and said, "I see you're all trying to figure out how to do the next step on balancing the budget." I replied, "Yes, that's right. And unlike last time, we'd love to have your help. We'd like to get Republicans votes for this because it's an important American effort. It's not really a partisan effort. We'll have disagreements over taxes and cutting programs. We know that. But we really need to do this for the sake of the country and the people." And he said, "Look, Dick, just like I told you last time, I'm not going to be for this. None of us are on the Republican side. You won the election. You won the presidency. You've got a majority in Congress. This is your problem. You have to do it with votes on just your side alone."

As a result, we knew we had an uphill climb. Even within our own caucus, many Democrats reacted badly to the knowledge that he was going to oppose it and that the Republicans wouldn't give us one vote. They kept asking me, "Why are we doing this? Why do we have to do this? The budget, the big budget deficit was really created right after the Reagan Presidency. We don't want to feel like we're the cleanup crew after they've had a great party — politically and economically." But I said, "That's why we're here. You got elected to do the right thing for the American people. You got elected to be a public servant, and you can't just worry about re-election holding power. I think if you if you go home and explain these votes to people and earn their trust — and you stay in close touch — you can probably get through this and survive your election."

The difficulties we faced resided on both sides of the Federal Income Statement. Balancing the budget involved not only cutting a lot of programs, but also raising taxes — particularly the gasoline tax — which financed the Highway Trust Fund. My goal was to raise it by ten cents a gallon.

I approached every member of the caucus and said, "Look, I need nearly everyone's vote on this. Can you vote to raise the gasoline tax? Maybe 9 or 10 cents?" And most replied that they couldn't support it as they feltcertain it would cost them their seat.

When I asked them why, they would answer, "Well, that's the one part of the package that my opponent would select. And they'd run TV ads saying, you know, Congressman X voted to raise your gasoline tax. They wouldn't say how much. They would just say you voted to raise the gasoline tax. People hate tax increases."

And I then would ask them, "How are we going to build the infrastructure of the country? You can't. Money doesn't come out of thin air. You've got to pay for these programs. It's an investment in the future of the economy and the country. It builds jobs. It solves problems. Think of our factories that now feature just-in-time manufacturing. They've got deliveries being made over the highway system every second of every day. If the highways are dysfunctional and they can't get the material there when they need it, companies are going to leave America. They're going to go somewhere where they can get cheap labor."

I then shared a story about a visit I made to a big Chrysler plant in my district where the manager said, "Dick, if you don't get this highway interchange fixed right near our plant, we're going to move the plant somewhere else in the country or out of the country." I asked why the interchange was so important, and he said, "We have just-in-time manufacturing. That interchange is ancient. It doesn't work. Our trucks are backed up for miles trying to get into this plant every minute of every day and night, and it makes our factory dysfunctional. We cannot function economically unless that's fixed."

After explaining all this to the members, I figured that I might be able to get the necessary votes for a three-cent increase. So, we went to bat for it on the floor just as we had in 1990. I had no idea if we were going to be able to pass it. I had worked on every member to try to get their votes. About thirty of them would not even tell me what they were going to do, and it didn't take much dot-connecting to assume that this meant that they were going to vote against it. I had to balance this against what I estimated to be a swing vote of approximately fifteen that would determine the outcome of the bill.

As was typically the case in these circumstances, I repeatedly delayed the vote because the worst outcome was to bring it to the floor and see it fail. Finally, the President called me and said, "Dick, we've got to go. Time is running out. It's getting late in the year. We're just never going to get this done." And I said, "I can't assure you that we're going to pass it at the moment." He understood.

"We'll all keep calling people, keep talking to people in person," I said. He said, "but you've just got to run the vote." So, with Speaker Foley's ascent, I called the bill up on the floor. We went out on the floor — always an electric moment when there is a tough, hotly contested vote on the docket. You have butterflies in your stomach. Your heart skips a beat.

Toward the end of the voting roll call, four Southern members approached me in the back of the Chamber, and I begged for their support. I arranged a phone call with Al Gore for one of them, Bill Clinton for another one. Both put the full press on.

Finally, when the vote closed, two of the Southerners had voted yes and two had voted no. When all the ballots were counted, it ended in a tie, which, according to House Rules, means the bill fails.

It is important to note that while the first ballot ended in a tie, there were a number of members — particularly on the Democratic side — who did not weigh in on the matter. In fact, in selected cases, I encouraged this. Many of these new representatives wanted us to succeed but felt they couldn't lend their vote to the cause. I told them simply not to vote. "Please wait till the end," I said, "and see where we are, and if we need your vote. You can vote the way you need to politically, but if we need your vote, I don't want you to commit and have to change it because that would really be embarrassing. So just hold out."

So, when first ballot ended up in a tie, I looked around the room to see if anyone I could cajole remained on the floor. There was only one left: Marjorie Margolies, who had been newly elected by a razor-thin margin in Pennsylvania's 13th District which covers suburban Philadelphia. At the time, she was married to former Congressman Ed Mevzinsky with whom she raised eleven children, many of whom she adopted from under-developed countries.

Prior to the floor session, she told me, "If I have to vote for this, I lose."

"I know, we'll do everything we can to help you," I replied.

But when I saw that she hadn't voted and she looked pale and like she was going to pass out, I went over to her and I said, "Marjorie, this is it. You have to help us. You have to do this. Your vote will put us over the top. And this is not about the Democratic Party. It's not about Bill Clinton. It's not even about you or me — it's about the country! That's what we got elected to do, to take tough votes. Even if the price is losing our election. That's what the job is about."

She issued a deep sigh, and she walked down the aisle. Even back then, the House used an electronic ballot, but any member who held back their decision and then decided to vote had to do so physically by picking up a red or green card, signing it, and handing it to the clerk.

The whole house was on the floor. Everybody was watching as Marjorie marched down the aisle.

The Republicans knew exactly what I had been talking to her about. They knew exactly what her situation was. And when she plopped down the green card, the Republicans stood in the aisles, waved their hands and began singing, "Bye-Bye, Marjorie." They knew that she was probably going to lose her seat in the 1994 election.

They ended up being right, but she was defeated because she did the right thing. After she left Congress, she joined the faculty of the Political Science Department at the University of Pennsylvania. Every year she'd bring her class to Washington. She would always call me before they got there and ask me to visit with them. And I always said yes because I really loved this woman for what she was willing to do.

So, when she would bring the class, I would always start by saying, "I'm really proud of your professor. She is my hero of democracy."

Meanwhile, the other big issue with which we were contending at the time was crime, which was on the rise across the United States particularly in large metropolitan areas. The President felt strongly that we needed to beef up the police effort in cities, which was needed then, and frankly, I believe is still needed now. To address this, the President conceived the Community Oriented Policing Service (COPS program), that, since its enactment in 1994, has provided more than fourteen billion dollars in funding for state and local law enforcement agencies.

I thought that this was a great idea, as local police forces never have enough adequate money for recruitment and training. Moreover, I believed then, as I do now, that a physical "walking" presence — policemen and women on the streets — is an important crime deterrent. When law enforcement personnel do nothing more than ride around in their cars and never interact directly with the people, opportunities are lost. Opportunities such enlisting the citizenry to really know their neighborhoods, involve themselves in the community, and help guide young people away from bad choices that can ruin their lives and those of others.

Both the President and the Vice President were also particularly interested in gun control. They wanted to institutionalize background checks, and, more importantly, to ban assault weapons. We just couldn't understand how any hunter — or any person interesting in owning rifles or pistols for legitimate purposes — needed an automatic firing assault weapon that can only be used in in military contexts to wound or kill.

We included both the COPS Program and Gun Control legislation in the early versions of our bill. Not surprisingly, we suffered huge blowback from the National Rifle Association and its constituents. They made the argument that anything even hinting of incremental restrictions on firearms was a wholesale threat to the Second Amendment. The NRA's feeling has always been that any gun restrictions of any kind were tantamount to "the camel sticking his nose under the tent," and that restrictions would beget more restrictions until all such weapons were under the complete control of the Federal Government.

Therefore, we knew right away that we had an uphill climb on Gun Control. Prior to the vote, I met with Clinton and Gore to inform them of my challenges on the floor. I said, "Boy, we're really struggling to get the votes for this, and the gun stuff is a big part of it. If we get the cops and some of the other provisions we had in the bill, that's probably enough."

But they were adamant that an assault weapons ban had to be part of the package. As it was something of a third rail issue, and to sweeten the pot for politically threatened members, we put a ten-year sunset clause on the ban. It was very close, but in the end we were able to achieve passage.

None of us understood at the time just how politically sensitive the issue was. I found out firsthand, when during the next Congressional election cycle, my opponent had distributed bumper stickers saying: "Ban Gephardt, Not Guns." In that time-honored door-to-door campaign, I felt the heat of my constituents. When I went to the home of a union guy I knew, he greeted me by saying, "Oh, Gephardt, I love you. You're the best. You represent us working people. Your dad was a union member. I'm a Teamster."

"I'm for everything that you've ever done in Congress. I'm an avid supporter. Would you let me have my son come out and take a picture with you? Would you take it? Let me take a picture of you and my son. I'm so thrilled that you're here."

He introduced his son and we took the picture. Afterwards, he said, "This is really something to have you here. But, you know, I can't vote for you this time."

"Why not?" I asked.

And he said: "I got a letter from the NRA and I'm an NRA member and I'm a hunter, and the letter said vote against Dick Gephardt because he will take your guns away."

I told him that this just wasn't true. I had only voted for an assault weapon ban and background checks, which he thought was sensible. I said, "I used to hunt with my dad. I would never take away your Second Amendment rights. That's ridiculous."

I could see the confusion on his face, and then he showed me the NRA letter, which sure enough was both inaccurate and over the top. It contained a headline that stated: "Vote against Dick Gephardt. He will take your guns away." I reiterated the facts of my arguments and promised him that I had no interest in any additional action relating to the 2nd Amendment.

When I could see I was not changing his mind, I finally said, "I appreciate your concern on this, but I have to keep going door-to-door. I hope you can still vote for me this fall."

He asked if he could walk with me so we could discuss this some more. I said, "Sure," and I made the same explanation when I came off each porch. At the end of the block, he said he was satisfied that I wouldn't vote to take away his guns and would vote for me despite the letter from the NRA.

I could not do that with every NRA Member, which is one of the things that makes single issue organizations such as the NRA so powerful. They hammer away at a delicate issue and will often resort to spreading disinformation. This is one of the thorniest challenges of democracy and the legislative process.

One way or the other, we had succeeded in passing a Crime Bill of which I am very proud. We pressed on to other issues. Hillary Clinton had been working with us to pull together a big health care reform bill. She did yeoman work on it. But I had a sense that we'd gone too far with our plans and that the concept was to aggressive and broad to have any hope of passage.

One day, Bob Dole called me, and said, "Dick, we won't get any votes for what Hillary and you all are talking about. It's too much — too complicated. But frankly, if you just change a few items — narrow the scope a bit — it might work."

In retrospect, he was pitching the health care plan that Mitt Romney as Governor had passed in Massachusetts, and which in my opinion later formed the blueprint for Obamacare.

I brought Dole's recommendations to the White House where I spoke with Bill, Hillary, and Ira Magaziner, the lead advisor to White House's health-care reform task force (since the Clinton White House Years, he headed up the Clinton Foundation's Health Care Access Initiative). I related what Senator Dole had told me and suggested that if we accepted his recommendations, we could probably get a bill passed. But the Clintons' balked, feeling that we had gone too far to make the contemplated compromises.

I went back to Dole and told him that the White House wouldn't move. This stymied the initiative so much that we couldn't even move it from the Commerce Committee to the floor, and it forced me to admit to the President that we just couldn't get it done. In my view, this was a real shame because I believe we could have achieved a bipartisan health care bill — a necessary component for any major legislative initiative. If a bill passes with only the support of the Majority party, as we learned after the 2010 passage of Obamacare, then the other side will spend its time in opposition to its core. By contrast, with bipartisan legislation, everyone aligns to make what was passed work and to improve it as necessary.

Though I didn't know it or expect it at the time, the failed health-care initiative marked a fitting end to my tenure as Majority Leader of the United States House of Representatives. The 1994 Congressional Election played out in such a way that, for the first time in forty years, Congress flipped from Democratic to Republican control.

As history shows, Newt Gingrich was the driving force behind this change. He had the Speaker's role in his crosshairs and was moving heaven and earth to achieve his objectives. It worked. When the dust settled, the Republicans had picked up eight Senate Seats and an astonishing fifty-four in the House. Even Speaker Foley lost his district in Washington State.

It was a gigantic defeat for the Democratic Party, in part I think because we had made some moves that I believe were very positive for the country, but highly unpopular politically. We faced additional headwinds owing to a historical trend under which a new president's party tends to lose seats in the subsequent midterm.

The national mood had changed. The citizenry was feeling the pinch on our earlier budgetary efforts. We pressed forward with, "Don't Ask, Don't Tell," paving the way for gays to serve openly in the military.

In the 103rd Congress, my role switched from Majority to Minority Leader. After the rout, I invited Newt Gingrich and his wife to my house in Virginia in an effort to establish the best possible working relationship with the incoming Speaker. I assured him that I wanted to work with him as effectively as possible. After dinner I said to him: "Newt, congratulations. You did an incredible thing here in winning the house after forty years in the minority. How did you do it?"

His one-word answer? "Money."

He told me that in previous election cycles, Republicans and Democrats raised money only at the party level. In addition, funds were limited to what is called "hard money," which implies limits on individual contribution amounts. At the time, I believe the cap was fixed at one thousand dollars. He told me that he had found a loophole around these constraints, allowing for the sourcing and use of "soft money."

He said, "In the last six months before the election, I raised thirty-five million dollars, and I spread it around in the races in which we thought we had the best chance. And, lo and behold, we pulled out a victory."

I listened carefully and formed new ideas for methods needed to establish and retain a legislative majority.

I did not look forward to January 3, 1995.

CHAPTER 8

Life in the Minority

O n January 4, 1995, I had the singular experience of handing the gavel of the Speaker of the House to Newton L. Gingrich of Georgia — the first Republican to hold that office since Joseph W. Martin, Jr. (Republican, Massachusetts) passed over the reins to Sam Rayburn (Democrat, Texas) in 1955.

So, on January 4, 1995, before I handed the Speaker's gavel over to Newt Gingrich, I made the following speech to the House of Representatives:

"First, I want to thank you Democratic colleagues for your support and confidence. I noted that we were a little short, but I appreciate your friendship and support.

When you carry the mantle of progress, there is precious little glory in defeat. But sometimes we spend so much time lionizing the winners and labeling the losers, we lose sight of the victory we all share in this crown jewel of democracy.

This is a day to celebrate a power that belongs not to any party, but to the people, no matter the margin, no matter the majority.

All across the world — from Bosnia to Chechnya — people lay down their lives for the kind of voice we take for granted. Too often the transfer of power is an act of pain and carnage, not one as we see today of peace and decency.

But here in the House of Representatives for 219 years, longer than any democracy in the world, we heed the people's voice with peace and civility and respect.

Each and every day, on this very floor, we echo the hopes and dreams of our people, their fears and their failures, their abiding belief in a better America.

We may not all agree with today's changing of the guard. We may not like it, but we enact the people's will with dignity and honor and pride. In that endeavor, there can be no losers and there can be no defeat.

Of course, in the 104th Congress, there will be conflict and compromise. Agreements will not always be easy — agreements sometimes not even possible.

However, while we may not agree on matters of party and principle, we all abide with the will of the people.

That is reason enough to place our good faith and our best hopes in your able hands."

With outgoing Speaker Tom Foley having lost his seat in the preceding election (becoming the first Speaker to lose a Congressional re-election bid), it felt as though a new regime had emerged. I didn't know the precise contours of Newt's legislative priorities, but having won his position based in large part upon his "Contract with America" program (described in the preceding chapter), I had what I believed was a pretty good introductory roadmap of his agenda.

My first challenge as Democratic Minority Leader (the first time the Democrats were in the minority in 40 years), was to establish a process within the Democratic Caucus to achieve consensus on the various policies or legislative vehicles the new Republican Majority would assert in the coming two years.

In the past, the leadership of the Democratic Caucus was just four people. I decided that leadership group should be expanded to 60 Representatives representing all of the various views within the Party and all of the varied parts of the country.

I asked the newly appointed group for one simple thing: I wanted them to meet together every night we were in session at 5 p.m. for two hours to discuss all the issues we would have to confront over the next two years.

The idea to establish this group and process came from my long-held belief that for groups of humans to be effective, it is necessary to meet in person, talk, listen, and try to reach decisions that would be superior to those that any one of us could devise alone.

I stated often to the group, "None of us knows everything; we have to listen to one another because only then can we understand and benefit from everyone's unique knowledge and experience."

This process never failed to achieve consensus in the group. We had many difficult meetings with angry disagreements, and sometimes people would leave the room in anger and bitter disagreement.

But they always returned. We all learned from those disagreements and eventually achieved compromise that allowed a consensus to emerge.

Then we could interact with our Republican colleagues with one voice so that we could work to reach an overall consensus more efficiently in the House of Representatives.

The work of a member of Congress requires time, patience, listening skills, and respect for everyone. Without that, the group of 535 (Congress) cannot function or carry out its responsibilities.

The first issue we had to confront was the Federal Budget. Central to "The Contract" was a commitment to balance the Federal Budget, an issue rising in importance in those days. So much so, that I believe this pledge was critical to the Republicans' having won the House in in 1994. There was true angst among the electorate about budget deficits at the time. And this angst was present even though we had made extraordinary progress toward balancing the budget under President George H W Bush and President Clinton. But the full positive impact of those budget efforts will still yet to be realized.

Thus, the 104th Congress began with a huge dust up about Federal expenditures. The Republican spending bill featured a range of budget cuts to which President Clinton and the Democratic Caucus objected. As was his prerogative, on June 8th, Clinton vetoed that spending bill — his first-ever use of that tool in the Presidential Arsenal.

Consistent with his style, Gingrich went nuclear and threatened to shut down the Federal Government. In an effort to resolve the impasse, the President convened a meeting with the Leaders of both Congressional branches: specifically, Speaker Gingrich, Senate Majority Leader Bob Dole, and the Minority Leaders on our side — Tom Daschle and me.

Vice President Gore was also in attendance.

Clinton spoke for the Democrats while Gingrich led the discussion for the GOP contingent. (Senator Dole, as I recall, was a more passive participant, perhaps because he was preparing his 1996 Presidential run and didn't want to lead what he feared was a politically controversial position.)

As they were discussing the specifics of their disagreements, Newt looked at Clinton and said:

"You know, the problem here is you've got a gun to my head called the veto. I need a gun to your head. And let me tell you what it is. I can shut the government down and that's what we're going to do."

The meeting broke up shortly thereafter. Nobody knew quite what to say.

And after that, Clinton took me over in a corner of the Oval Office asked: "Do you think he's really going to do this?"

I said, "You bet he's going to do it. This is what they ran on, and this is what they're intending to do."

I continued, "Look, this is now a communications battle. They're going to try to go out and say why they did this, and we need to be in front of TV cameras. You and Gore and all of us — the leaders in the House and Senate need to be in front of cameras and reporters every day saying this is not the way our government works. The Constitution says that Congress sends bills to the president for his approval or disapproval. If he disapproves of a bill and vetoes it, there's a very set procedure in our Constitution and in our process, and that is you don't shut the government down. You prepare another bill and send it down to the President to see if he'll sign that. If he doesn't sign that, he vetoes again and you put together a third bill. You just keep going until you resolve the conflict and you don't shut the government down. There's no justification for doing that."

Clinton liked the idea. So, we talked about it in public forums every day. But the shutdown, in fact more than one, happened anyway. The first began on November 14, 1995 and ended on the 19th. Clinton was forced to suspend operations across several Federal departments, and to furlough about 80,000 Federal workers

Though unfortunate, this worked to our political advantage. The press was all over the shutdown. They listened to our arguments and supported our ideas, ultimately agreeing that defunding the government was not the right way to resolve budget disputes and not the way the system was designed to operate. The mounting pressure (combined with the tepid support he was receiving from Dole) forced Newt back to the negotiating table. After five days of shutdown, he agreed to a temporary spending bill and to a resumption of negotiations.

Discussions indeed resumed, but we had little in the way of progress to show for them. World events intervened. On November 4th, Yitzhak Rabin, Prime Minister of Israel and winner of the preceding year's Nobel Peace Prize — along with Palestinian Leader Yasser Arafat and Shimon Peres, who was both the predecessor and successor to Rabin as Israeli Prime Minister — was gunned down by an extremist opposed to the Israeli/Palestinian treaty that had garnered Rabin the award.

President Clinton was a close friend of Rabin's and always a staunch supporter of Israel. He personally attended the funeral. He invited the four Congressional leaders to join him — including yours truly. It was a very moving service, and Rabin's loss was a great tragedy for Israel and the world.

When we returned, upon our landing Air Force One at St. Andrews Air Force Base, and for reasons unknown to me, the Secret Service only permitted the President to exit the front of the plane, asking the rest of us to use the back exit. This annoyed the easily roused Speaker of the House to no end, and he complained loudly to the Press about what he believed was an affront to him and his office.

On November 16th, The New York Daily News published a front-page caricature of Gingrich wearing a diaper, with a caption that read: "Newt's Tantrum: He closed down the government because Clinton made him sit at the back of plane." The caption was slightly inaccurate (we were only asked to exit through the rear), but the image followed Newt for the rest of his career.

Unable to resist sweet temptation, we ordered a big blow up of the cover page and pasted it to the back of the Speaker's chair in the main chamber of the House. Newt was livid, of course.

And if you asked him, he'd probably admit that his early time as Speaker was filled with some frustration. Beyond the bad press discussed above, David Bonior (a Democrat from Michigan who held the number two spot in the Democratic Caucus during my time as Minority Leader), began to push for an ethics investigation against Gingrich. Ironically, the charge was very similar to the one Newt had laid upon Jim Wright that forced the latter to resign from Congress.

Specifically, the allegations involved Newt's publication of a book, sold en masse to his donors, all for his personal financial gain. The investigation resulted in a (very rare) Congressional reprimand against the Speaker in 1997.

As the investigation unfolded, Newt called me into his office and said, "You know you that all this stuff that Bonior is bringing up about me is bullshit. And what you need to do is to stop this ethics investigation."

I replied "Newt, you know, I'm not I'm not all powerful in the Caucus. I can't tell the Bonior what to do. It is what it is, and there's nothing I can do to stop it." And he looked me in the eye and said, very forcefully:

"Well, you're going to be sorry."

The very next week, ethics charges were filed against all the members of the Democratic leadership, including me. They were all demonstrably false.

The charge against me was that I had purchased a house in the Outer Banks in North Carolina that I was renting out for personal financial gain to Washington lobbyists.

None of this was true. And all of it was dismissed by the Ethics Committee. This type of personal attack in political settings dates back to the formation of human government itself, and few who enter the political arena escape unscathed. Bonior was responding to what Gingrich had done to Jim Wright. Gingrich was responding to what Bonnier was doing to him. All so circular. All so destructive.

All the above offered a salacious backdrop to the whole budget mess. The temporary appropriations bill that we passed on November 19th expired on December 16th with no resolution to the underlying dispute in sight. As the reader may remember (or guess), Newt's response was to shut down the government. Again.

The second discontinuation lasted twenty-one days and was of much larger magnitude. This time, we were forced to furlough two hundred eighty-four thousand government employees. Again, we took our case to the press and the public, reminding all concerned that if a president vetoes a bill, the proper approach is to redraft it and send it back for his consideration. But that isn't what happened.

On balance, it was clear to us that the shutdown strategy was working against the Republicans and in our favor. This was a cause of great concern to Newt. As the days of the shutdown extended, however, it was clear to both sides that we needed to resolve the issue and quickly.

Not helping matters, oddly, was the weather. Between January 6th and 8th of 1996, a blizzard dumped four feet of snow on Washington. I remember trying to get to a meeting in the Oval Office with Newt and the other leaders. It took a whole day to have the Capitol Police pick me up in Virginia, where I lived, and transport me to the White House.

In any event, after twenty-one days of shutdown, we were finally able to work out a bill that began to deal with some of Newt's issues. It featured deep, long-term spending cuts. In my view, it was the culmination of work begun under the George H. W. Bush Administration to balance the federal budget. By September 1996, we finally obtained a bipartisan consensus for a '97 budget.

As is topical even today, the final bill involved a process called Budget Reconciliation under which the Senate and House each compile a plan—outside of the protocols of the filibuster (and therefore requiring only fifty-one Senate votes)—and then reconcile the differences through negotiation. The objective was to balance the budget by 2002, but we were able to achieve the goal much earlier. As it turned out, the Federal budget not only registered as a surplus in 1998, but also for the subsequent four years.

By 2002, though, we were back in deficit, with the associated shortfalls growing in alarming proportion to this day. A major source of the increased spending pressure derived from the Health Care Sector. Our work in 1997 featured deep cuts to Medicare providers who pushed hard to reverse them.

Throughout, electoral politics loomed large. After losing the House in '94, we set our sights on recapturing it two years later. We knew at the time that a big driver of Republican success was in their fundraising edge, and specifically our inability to match the Republicans on the soft money side.

Therefore, I spent a good deal of my time in '95 and '96 traveling around the country raising money for the Democratic Congressional Campaign Committee. With soft money now at our disposal, our balances rose dramatically. While quaint by today's standards, the effort produced $25 – $30 million, an astonishing amount at the time.

We needed to win a net twenty-six seats in order to retake the House in '96. Unfortunately, we managed to pick up three. Of course, in addition to restoring the chamber to Democratic control, I will admit to having my sights set on perhaps becoming Speaker. But honestly, that was secondary in my mind to the former mission.

In any event, we failed. However, I do think we moved the needle in our direction, picking up some seats and supporting Clinton's re-election by a fairly wide margin. In retrospect, I believe that the budget battles and government shutdown worked in our favor. And the irony is that Clinton's opponent in the '96 election, Bob Dole, was ambivalent about Newt's shut-down tactics.

So, I do think we helped re-elect the President, who had a very interesting time of it in his second term.

However, that is the subject of the next chapters.

CHAPTER 9

"Here, Sir, the People Govern"

The House of Representatives operates in a never-ending political cycle. As mentioned above, having failed to win back the House in '96, we began to turn our attention to '98.

As mentioned, on January 22, 1997, the House voted to reprimand Speaker Gingrich. The vote tally told the story: 395 for the reprimand and 28 against. In addition to the public censure, Congress imposed a fine of $300,000.

His reaction, perhaps not unnaturally, was one of petulance and anger. But the wheels of government continued to spin. We did manage to balance the budget, but the overall tone of the chamber was tense and less than conducive to effective governance.

1997 faded into 1998, and, with the latter, came the next midterm election cycle. As the calendar turned, I found myself more and more optimistic about our chances to recapture the House.

Then, the Monica Lewinsky story exploded — not only in Washington but across the country. At that point, with respect to mid-terms, instead of feeling confident we could win, I was worried that we might lose 100 seats.

The Scandal broke on January 17, 1998. Sometime during that month, a key player in the drama (Linda Tripp) forwarded recorded conversations between herself and Ms. Lewinsky to Ken Starr, a

Congressionally appointed Independent Counsel, who was already investigating the Clintons about matters ranging from the mysterious death of White House Advisor Vince Foster to the couple's business dealings during The President's tenure as Governor of Arkansas (the so-called Whitewater Scandal).

Starr immediately turned almost the entirety of his attention to the Lewinsky matter.

The Republicans were under the stewardship of House Minority Leader Tom Delay, a Texas Republican who was eventually charged and convicted of campaign finance fraud. The conviction was ultimately overturned. With Starr's support, he charged ahead with the investigation.

Though I could see that the process would move forward inevitably, I did what I could to try to stop it, but knew nothing would work. At one time I met with Gingrich and said: "Newt, do you really think this is the right remedy for this problem? Couldn't you reprimand the President or some way pass something that would be short of impeachment, but which would point out is improper conduct?"

Newt said, "Well, it's not my idea, it's DeLay pushing it in the caucus. I really don't want to go ahead with it, but he's insisting and the majority of the caucus really wants to do this. So there's nothing I can do to stop it or even slow it down."

I suspect that Newt took some satisfaction in giving me the same reply I offered him when he asked me to stop the ethics investigation against him. One way or another, I spent the next several weeks meeting with the Democrats on the House Judiciary Committee, who would be responsible for Clinton's defense, on a daily basis.

Among other things, this meant that I was not out there raising money for the '98 Congressional Campaign.

Memories of this episode faded into history, but it was beyond dramatic. For most of 1998 and into early 1999, the nation and the world was riveted by the drama.

Up to that point, only one president, Andrew Johnson, had ever been impeached, and he was not removed from office. Of course, another, Richard Nixon, resigned in advance of an impeachment proceeding that was pending against him.

The legal grounds for impeachment are embedded in Article II, Section 4 of the Constitution, with the following language:

"The Constitution gives Congress the authority to impeach and remove the President, Vice President, and all federal civil officers for treason, bribery, or other high crimes and misdemeanors."

Under the law, the House of Representatives first considers whether the President's behavior meets the associated legal standard, and, if the House believes that it does, it brings an impeachment action that is the political equivalent of an indictment. The action then moves to Committee, and if approved, to a vote on the floor.

If it passes, the case then is taken up by the Senate, who acts as a jury in the proceedings. The Chief Justice of the Supreme Court presides. House "Managers" present their case, which, in order to effect removal, must pass by a two-third (67 seat) Senatorial majority.

It is a process which by its very nature, can lend itself to abuse by either party using it, among other evils, to remove an elected official without the need for a vote by the electorate.

Three factors embedded in the law serve as mitigants.

First, as mentioned above, is the need for a two-third majority to achieve conviction. This is an exceedingly high bar, virtually assuring that a single party cannot ram through such an action for pure political reasons (while one can envision a party with a two-thirds majority in the Senate, it's highly unlikely that such an imbalance would transpire while the opposing party held the presidency).

Second, the Constitution sets a clear legal standard for what rises to "high crimes and misdemeanors."

Finally, there is the political process itself. As detailed below, the American people are by and large predisposed against impeachment, believing — in addition to the disruption it brings about — that unless the behavior in question clearly meets the Constitutional standard, it is an act that runs against the popular will as registered in the ballot box.

All these factors were under consideration in the Clinton impeachment. For these reasons (even though the Republicans held a fifty-five to forty-five majority), it was truly a stretch to envision a scenario where sixty-seven senators would vote to remove him from office.

As related in additional detail below, both the Perjury and Obstruction of Justice charges failed by a wide margin. I believe one reason for this was the political fallout. The '98 midterm elections took place as the drama was unfolding to its critical stage, and the Republicans (who everyone was expecting to run the table) actually lost seats in the House.

Yes, that was how it played out. But when the issue first emerged, I was very worried that we were going to lose a majority of the Democrats on the Committee — as well as the vote itself — if the initiative made it to the floor of the House. To help stem the tide, we hired Abbe Lowell, who was a very competent criminal attorney in Washington. I must have met with him twenty-five or thirty times.

Just as we were developing our defense, we learned that the redoubtable Larry Flynt of Hustler Magazine was about to break a story about the extramarital affairs of Bob Livingston, a Louisiana

Republican who was a leader of the impeachment crusade, and who was in line to replace Newt as Speaker of the House. In one of the more dramatic moments of my Congressional career, on December 19, 1998, just as the Clinton Impeachment debate was about to begin in the House, Livingston resigned not only his leadership position, but also his seat in Congress.

I applauded Livingston's consistency, and in one of my more memorable speeches (delivered on the same day shortly after his resignation), I said:

"Mr. Speaker and members of the House, I stood on this floor yesterday and implored all of us to say that the politics of slash-and-burn must end. I implored all of you that we must turn away from the politics of personal destruction and return to the politics of values.

It is with that same passion that I say to all of you today that the gentleman from Louisiana, Bob Livingston, is a worthy and good and honorable man.

I believe his decision to retire is a terrible capitulation to the negative forces that are consuming our political system and our country.

And I pray with all my heart that he will reconsider this decision.

Our founding fathers created a system of government of men, not of angels. No one standing in this House today can pass a Puritanical test of purity that some are demanding that our elected leaders take.

If we demand that mere mortals live up to this standard, we will see our seats of government lay empty, and we will see the best, most able people unfairly cast out of public service.

We need to stop destroying imperfect people at the altar of an unobtainable morality.

We need to start living up to the standards which the public, in its infinite wisdom, understands that imperfect people must strive towards, but too often fall short.

We are now rapidly descending into a politics where life imitates farce. Fratricide dominates our public debate and America is held hostage to tactics of smear and fear.

Let all of us here today say no to resignation, no to impeachment, no to hatred, no to intolerance of each other, and no to vicious self-righteousness.

We need to start healing. We need to start binding up our wounds. We need to end this downward spiral which will culminate in the death of representative democracy.

I believe this healing can start today by changing the course we've begun.

This is exactly why we need this today to be bipartisan. This is why we ask for the opportunity to vote on a bipartisan censure resolution, to begin the process of healing our nation and healing our people.

We are on the brink of the abyss. The only way we stop this insanity is through the force of our own will.

The only way we stop this spiral is for all of us to finally say—ENOUGH!

Let us step back from the abyss and let's begin a new politics of respect and fairness and decency which raises what has come before.

May God have mercy on this Congress and may Congress have the wisdom and the courage and the goodness to save itself today."

This speech addressed a persistent threat that is always present in politics. If politics is a substitute for violence, there is always a temptation for politicians to use character assassination of their opponents rather than articulating differences over policy and vision.

Now this phenomena dominates almost all political campaigns so the public is presented a steady drumbeat of very negative messages from both sides that include a lot of character assassination.

The net result of these constant negative personal attacks over the modern means of communication (television and social media) is destroying any respect or trust the public has in any public servant. Ultimately, this will cause the destruction of self-government.

To give an analogy, an Anheuser Busch executive once told me if beer companies start advertising that competitor products contain poison, and their competitors retaliate in kind, consumers will stop buying any beer.

In any event, we had the vote the same day. And the House voted to impeach, though most Democrats voted no. Meanwhile, as all of this was transpiring, the United States and the United Kingdom were in the midst of a four-day Iraqi bombing operation. But we impeached anyway. President Clinton called me immediately afterwards. He wanted to hold a press conference, but I thought it was a bad idea.

He insisted, and so a contingent that included both Mr. and Ms. Clinton, Vice President Gore, Minority Leader Tom Daschle (Democrat, South Dakota) and I, stepped in front of the podium to make statements and answer press questions. It was all very surreal. I didn't know what I was going to say, and don't remember what I said (if anything). But it was a really bad day for the country and certainly for President Clinton.

The process dragged on into the New Year. On February 9, 1999, the Senate voted to acquit the President on both counts against which he was charged: Perjury and Obstruction of Justice. Removal of a President (or any high office holder) requires a two-third majority (sixty-seven votes) in the Senate. The first charge garnered only fortyfive votes and the second an insufficient fifty.

It was over.

All of the events of 1998 marked the end of Newt's run as Speaker. My own read is that his caucus simply tired of him, and he understood it was time to move on.

And move on he did. In January 1999, he resigned his seat in the House of Representatives.

This left the Speakership open, and with Livingston having also removed himself from the running, the GOP's choices devolved to Tom DeLay (who I believe was instrumental in Newt's removal and had his eye fixed on the top spot himself) and Dennis Hastert (Republican, Illinois). The Caucus selected the latter, a former high school wrestling coach—in part, presumably, because they wanted quiet, calm, drama-free leadership. His was the longest run of any Republican in the role of Speaker (seven years), but the drama came later in 2015 when Hastert pled guilty to money laundering and child molestation.

As 1999 unfolded, we had disposed of the impeachment matter, Newt was gone, and it was time to turn the page in Washington. Inevitably, thoughts turned to the 2000 election. Clinton was riding pretty high having survived the impeachment and presiding over a surging economy.

Vice President Gore was gearing up for his own campaign and was a little concerned that I was contemplating a run of my own. I had no such intention; I figured it was legitimately Gore's time. But my friend and colleague, Bill Bradley, had other ideas. He approached me and asked me if I was going to run. When I responded in the negative, he told me that he himself was going to give it a shot because he believed that Gore needed to be challenged in the primaries.

I think that Bill thought a Gore candidacy would be seen as a de facto third Clinton term and that Vice President Gore shouldn't be handed the Democratic nomination without a primary contest.

Bill gave it a good go but faded before Iowa and New Hampshire. Gore won the nomination with relative ease.

The General Election, of course, was another story. It came down to a disputed outcome that the Supreme Court was ultimately called upon to settle.

This decision marked only the third time (but not the last) in history where the winner in the Electoral College majority lost the popular vote to his opponent (the others being Rutherford B. Hayes in 1876 and Benjamin Harrison in 1888).

We can therefore describe the 2000 Presidential Election as a tie, particularly as it applied to the sentiments of the Electorate. Importantly, the outcome may have been different (i.e., the election of Gore) had events not unfolded as they did since Florida's results were a statistical dead heat. There was the manual counting of votes in certain counties and numerous recounts. Ultimately, the Supreme Court –under enormous pressure from Tom Delay and the Republicans — stopped the process. This amounted to a de facto decision to declare Bush the winner based upon a 537-ballot margin out of nearly 6 million votes cast in Florida!

I find the number itself to be ironic. Bush won by precisely two more votes than the number of Senators and Representatives in Congress.

Meanwhile, during the process, everyone was on the edge of their seats. I remember sitting in my office one Sunday with Gore Campaign Manager Bill Daley, wondering whether the Supreme Could would take up the case. They were going to decide the issue that day. When they announced that they would indeed review the Republican petition to stop the recount, we decided to hold a press conference urging the process to continue. However, right then, we received the notice that the Court had ruled in favor of the Republican suit. They ordered the recounts stopped, and Florida certified the election in Bush's favor, awarding him the twenty-five electoral votes that put him over the top.

As a result, Daley and I had to determine our immediate next steps. The Court had awarded the election to Bush, but we hadn't spoken to Gore yet. So, we called him to get his take. Many of those around him had encouraged him to continue to the fight, but this was his decision alone to make. He took a day or two to reflect, and in the meantime, Daley and I held that press conference on December 9th in the shadow of the U.S. Capitol. In my remarks, I called for a continuation of the vote counting process, stressed the need to ensure that all ballots were included, and urged everyone to abide by the result once the process was finished.

The Republicans pushed hard against these arguments, and, in the end, prevailed. Gore decided to pack it in. On December 13, 2000, he conceded. It was a very moving speech, the last sections of which went as follows:

"I've seen America in this campaign, and I like what I see. It's worth fighting for and that's a fight I'll never stop.

As for the battle that ends tonight, I do believe as my father once said, that no matter how hard the loss, defeat might serve as well as victory to shape the soul and let the glory out.

So for me this campaign ends as it began: with the love of Tipper and our family; with faith in God and in the country I have been so proud to serve, from Vietnam to the vice presidency; and with gratitude to our truly tireless campaign staff and volunteers, including all those who worked so hard in Florida for the last thirty-six days.

Now the political struggle is over and we turn again to the unending struggle for the common good of all Americans and for those multitudes around the world who look to us for leadership in the cause of freedom.

In the words of our great hymn, "America, America": "Let us crown thy good with brotherhood, from sea to shining sea."

And now, my friends, in a phrase I once addressed to others, it's time for me to go."

His words ring with particular authenticity in the present time, especially when compared against the behavior of Donald Trump in the wake of his 2020 loss to Joe Biden. I will always admire Al Gore for being the patriot and human being that he is, and for giving up his dream of being President of the United States. He thought more of the greater good of the country than of his own interests.

And, in the end, that's what all public servants should be willing to do. The same can be said, as I described previously, of Marjorie Margolies Mezvinsky, who sacrificed her Congressional seat in her very first term to help us pass the Clinton budget in 1994.

Another good example of this behavior is what Mike Pence did on January 6, 2021. He showed the same selfless courage as Al Gore.

In all these instances, as well as countless others, we have benefitted from the blessings of public servants willing to sacrifice their careers and offices for the greater good of the nation. It hardly needs stating, but we can use as much of this type of public service ethic as we can secure — never more so than in current times where we are so polarized.

Early 2001 ushered in a new Republican president who enjoyed a narrow (seven seat) majority in the House. The Senate was split 50/50, with the GOP controlling the tie-breaking Vice Presidential vote. However, the latter was short lived. In May of 2001, Vermont Senator James Jeffords switched parties and joined the Democratic caucus in the Senate.

As a result, the government was split for most of that eventful year. I was still Minority Leader and intent on doing the best for my party, and more importantly, for the country.

The next two years, as described in the following chapter, were quite a ride.

CHAPTER 10

Troubles at Home and Away

A ll readers are presumably aware that the first year in the presidency of George W. Bush was a historic one, but it didn't necessarily set out to be that way. My impression is that as he entered the White House, he sought to set a modest tone and put forward a fairly limited policy agenda.

To the extent that this was the case, it was perhaps understandable. After a closely contested general election, the outcome of which required court intervention to settle, his goals were to establish himself firmly as president, and, if possible, to bring the country together.

All of this was probably wise. The more congenial attitude began when he formally became President-Elect with a call to Al Gore that Gore described as touching.

While his introductory policy goals were perhaps short of sweeping, he was intent on one thing: passing a tax cut against the opposition of me and the Democratic Caucus. We really believed that it was the wrong move, particularly in the wake of all the hard work we'd done with his father, and later with Bill Clinton, to finally balance the budget.

However, on June 7, 2001, The Economic Growth and Tax Reconciliation Relief Act of 2001 (EGTRRA) was signed into law. It was a sweeping U.S. tax reform package that lowered income tax brackets, put into place new limits on the estate tax, allowed for higher contributions into IRA accounts, and created new employer-sponsored retirement plans.

I believed at the time that this would lead us back into an extended deficit mess. Unfortunately, subsequently, I was proven correct. By 2002, we were in a shortfall of $158 billion that year — quaint by today's standards— and growing, with exponential force nearly every year. By 2020 it exceeded (and will continue to do so) $3 trillion. Looking back, however, I believe the process worked as intended by the Framers. Bush was President, and his party held comfortable majorities in both houses of Congress. As a matter of law, the tax cut was entirely legitimate.

As an economic strategy? Well, I'll let others decide.

All of this was prologue to 2001's seminal event: the terrorist attack of September 11th.

While the events and implications of that day have been rehashed ad infinitum, I will take the time to tell my version of the story. As Minority Leader, I had a unique window into what transpired.

The first impression that I will share is that the government had significant advance warning that something of this nature was likely to transpire. A warning that we — who were sworn to protect the safety of all Americans — had tragically failed to heed.

We simply did not pay sufficient attention to information dating back over many years.

There was the failed February 26, 1993, World Trade Center attack, during which terrorists planted bombs in the buildings' underground garage. Later that year (August 7th), our embassies in Kenya and Tanzania were bombed, killing 224 people including twelve Americans.

Three years later, the Iranians bombed the Khobar Towers Complex, a facility that housed a multi-national military coalition to protect a no-fly zone established by Clinton over Iraq. Nearly 500 people died, including nineteen members of the U.S. Air Force. President Clinton did respond to this by sending missiles into that eternal region of strife known as Afghanistan.

As the remainder of the century passed, members of our intelligence community were in accelerated receipt of information that the extremists were planning a bigger attack — this time on U.S. shores. We took in this information, but obviously didn't do enough to ward off the inevitable.

And the inevitable came to pass on September 11, 2001. At the moment the tragedy unfolded, I was meeting at the Capitol with my Congressional Leadership Group, working to hammer out a strategy for the 2002 budget negotiations.

There was a television in the conference room next to my office, but I couldn't see it from where I was sitting that morning. I noticed everyone else mesmerized by something on the screen and wondered why they wouldn't focus on the topic at hand. I soon realized that a plane had struck one of the Twin Towers, but in the moment, we assumed it was simply a light aircraft and an accident.

We continued with the meeting. Then the second plane hit, and almost at the same instant, the Capitol Police entered and told us we had to evacuate immediately.

They grabbed me and ran me out of the building, pushed me into our SUV, and drove away at least eighty miles an hour down the streets of D.C., back to my townhouse in Virginia. The police stayed to watch events unfold, and repeatedly said to me:

"We don't know what's going to happen. We don't know where you're going to go. We have to wait for orders from headquarters on what to do next."

Approximately an hour later, they got a call from the Capitol Police Headquarters summoning me there. That building is a few blocks north of the Capitol Building, which as we now know, was the target of the fourth plane. That attack was thwarted by a group of heroic passengers who overtook the hijackers. They lost their lives not by crashing into the Capitol Building, but rather in an unoccupied field in Stonycreek, PA.

God bless them.

When we arrived at police headquarters, we were informed that Vice President Dick Cheney and the Department of Defense had decided that we should implement the formal Government Survival Plan—a roadmap always in place to ensure at least the partial functioning of government in the event of, say, a nuclear attack.

The plan as it pertained to me (as one of the four Congressional Leaders) was to fly me in a helicopter to a remote location in Virginia.

So, I was ushered out onto the lawn of the Capitol and was greeted by four Black Hawk helicopters. The four Leaders were put into a separate aircraft, and we took off. I will never forget, as long as I live, the scene below me as I looked down and observed the Pentagon engulfed in flames and smoke. And then I realized that another plane hit the Pentagon itself — the headquarters for our military.

All I could think was that our Second World War enemies— Germany and Japan—would have given their eye teeth to be able to do something of this nature, particularly toward the end of the war. But even with huge armies of men and equipment, they couldn't pull this off.

By contrast, on 9/11, four anonymous terrorists armed with nothing more than hardware store weapons were able to launch a huge missile into the very nexus of our military operations. It was an obvious indication of how much technology, transportation, and mindsets had changed. Like Japanese Kamikaze Pilots, they were willing to sacrifice their lives to attack a center of American Government, on its home shores, in its Capitol city.

It was a terrifying moment to say the least — for me and everyone in the country. That it was a setback for the nation is beyond dispute. And it caused everyone to rethink the nature of what National Security is, what it should be, and how best to protect the people of the United States from this new form of menace.

At any rate, our helicopters transported us to a helipad at the base of a mountain in Virginia, the location and existence of which I was entirely unaware. From there, SUVs escorted us up the mountain where, unbeknownst to us, there was a Government Survival Plan military base.

We were there for a few hours, during which time (before the wide availability of cell phones) we repeatedly attempted to reach the White House. President Bush was sequestered inside of Air Force One, unable — per Central Command instructions — to land until every single plane in U.S. airspace had touched down.

We did stay in contact with Cheney, but didn't know where precisely where he was (presumably anywhere but Washington). We mountaineering Congressional Leaders remained in perpetual phone conversation with the Vice President and pressed him to authorize our return to Washington. Our pleas took the following form: members of Congress don't know where we are and are wandering around Washington without any information, with nothing to convey to their constituents, and no way to organize the powers of the legislature as part of the response. It's chaos.

Cheney held firm. He informed us that we could not return (as was the policy for the President) until we grounded every plane commercial or otherwise that was in operation at the time of the attack.

Eventually, the number of unaccounted for aircraft dwindled down to three — all of which had taken off from Europe.

In my opinion, one of the underappreciated elements of the 9/11 saga was the extraordinary work of the Federal Aviation Administration to empty the skies over the entire country—with no warning or opportunity to plan—in the space of a few short hours that day. More than four thousand commercial aircraft, and many, many thousand more private planes were all guided to earthbound safety by the FAA in less than a day's worth of sunlight.

It was a case where the government and the private sector worked together beautifully to achieve a very important goal. We rarely take any comfort from how well this country can work during real crisis.

Finally, Cheney summoned us back Washington after nightfall. They put us back on those choppers in the darkness. We flew back to the Capitol and were informed that many of the members were gathered on the steps of the East Front of the Capitol building. The four of us greeted everyone with hugs — so many hugs.

Then we held a press conference. Speaker Hastert and Senate Majority Leader Tom Daschle (Democrat, South Dakota—who became Majority leader that June after, as mentioned above, Jim Jeffords withdrew from the Republican Party and began caucusing with the Democrats and bestowing the majority to our side) did most of the talking. Not much of import was said. We were all still in shock—still in the dark.

There was an important moment at the end, however. All the members present began, in spontaneous fashion, to sing "God Bless America."

And that was the way it ended — in my judgment an important and historic moment. Members of Congress took that opportunity to say to the people that the country, your government, is still here. We've survived, and this great country will recover from this blow.

With all due respect to the fabulous Kate Smith, I cannot hear that song without thinking of that rendition — sung by the (mostly) bereft of musical talent Congress — on the Capitol steps in the twilight hours of September 11, 2001.

But it was then time to move on to deal with a new, more dangerous world that had changed in the flash of an eye. The Congressional Leadership met with the President and Vice President, first to download our feelings and impressions, and then to formulate a comprehensive plan of response. When it was my turn to speak, I said, very simply:

"Mr. President, the only thing that matters now is that we trust one another. There's no blame to be placed. There are no speeches to be given about who didn't do what. The truth is we all failed. You failed. We failed. The FBI failed. The CIA failed. Our military failed. This was a joint failure to keep the American people safe.

"And politics always gets into everything, and there will be a tendency for this group to blame that group and to try to place the blame away from themselves. There can be no room for that. We have to trust one another. We have to work together as best we can to solve the problems that we now face in making sure that something like this can never happen again."

At the end of the meeting, Bush came up to me told me that he really appreciated my statement. He then set up a schedule under which the six of us would meet in the Oval Office every Tuesday at 7 a.m. to discuss security issues designed to prevent future possible terrorist attacks. We all believed we had to do better to achieve our most important responsibility — keeping the American people safe.

I thought this was solid leadership on his part. He took our suggestions seriously and followed through on the schedule, often looping in individuals such as CIA Director George Tenet and National Security Advisor Condi Rice.

It was in those meetings that we came up with the policy of setting up of the Transportation Security Administration to provide security at the airports so that something like what had happened could never happen again. In addition, we enacted wide ranging legislation, including the Patriot Act (not widely known is that the name is actually an acronym for Providing Appropriate Tools Required to Intercept and Obstruct Terrorism).

I was very pleased with our cooperation and response, but not everyone felt that way. There has been a great deal of criticism, for instance, of Vice President Cheney — particularly the lengths to which he was willing to extend government power to root out potential threats with devices such as waterboarding and other forms of torture.

I think one can argue that in certain areas he went too far. But I understood his perspective based upon what we were confronting at the time. During those Tuesday morning meetings, we were in routine receipt of intelligence from the CIA and other agencies of the Defense Department that a second, larger attack was imminent, and that this time, it might involve nuclear weapons.

That was our greatest worry. None of us could possibly imagine anything worse than a post-9/11 nuclear attack on American shores. And there were so many ways that it could happen. For instance, a dirty bomb backpack explosion would be very difficult to guard in any comprehensive fashion. Large cities such as New York, Los Angeles, and Washington were particularly susceptible.

Around that time, we received some intelligence that Middle Eastern scientists may have provided nuclear technology IP to terrorist organizations. We received some signals that some scientists were suspected of giving these tools to the terrorists, and we took this very seriously.

Also, we realized how poorly informed we were about terrorist organizations in general and on al-Qaeda in particular. In order to fill this understanding gap, it was necessary to examine the dysfunctional root causes in countries like Saudi Arabia, where these organizations were formed. This was the birth nation of Osama bin Laden, and the home of fifteen out of the nineteen kamikaze terrorists who attacked us on 9/11. Bin Laden was the son of Saudi Royalty, a scion of great wealth, whose father built all the palaces for all the royal family in Saudi Arabia and the surrounding countries.

How could one of the sons of the regime become so bitterly hateful of his environment that he would seek to destroy it and everything he could within his visible universe? I believe the origins can be traced to the Saudi Royal Family and everything it stood for. I believe this was at the core of his animosity. Attacking the United States — the staunchest ally of the House of Saud — would do the trick. The House of Saud is protected everywhere and in all things. The United States, by contrast, allows and encourages freedom of movement for all. If you consider it from this perspective, we were sitting ducks.

All these impressions brought back memories of my visit to Riyadh early in my Congressional career. And as described in an earlier chapter, particularly the hours that the King dedicated to warning us of the terrorist threat to destroy the mosque in Mecca.

And then it came to me: the Royal Family was terrified of these groups and willing to go to great lengths to protect themselves. Their strategy was to shower terrorist groups with money as an inducement to attack others and not them. I think, though they guarded this secret carefully, the record would show that the Family provided significant funding to al-Qaeda and similar organizations and asked in return that they leave Saudi Arabia. As a result, Osama bin Laden went to Afghanistan, where he and others, backed by House of Saud capital, recruited and trained his troops.

It all presumably began in 1979 with the Iranian Revolution, a real wake-up call for them in terms of their worry about radicalism among Muslims. Instead of trying to reduce the influence of radical Islamists in their Country (which they succeeded in doing much later) they simply paid money to the radicals to divert the problem. Most damaging was that some of those funds wound up funding schools in other Islamic countries that have perpetuated radical thinking and behavior. Of late, fortunately, the Saudi royal family is taking steps to reduce radical, violent behavior in their Country and give their citizens more basic freedoms of thought and behavior.

But towards the end of 2001, George Bush begun to focus on Iraq and his worry that Saddam Hussein either had or was trying to acquire weapons of mass destruction, including nuclear devices. And he wasn't alone. The CIA was worried, and Cheney was concerned that the technology that could threaten the United States could wind up in the hands of al-Qaeda or other terrorist groups.

It was apparent early on the direction of Bush's thinking. And, as the Iraq dialogue took sharper focus in our Tuesday meetings, I said to him:

"Mr. President, if you're thinking of just doing something to get rid of Saddam Hussein because he's a really bad guy, I'm not for it."

He was clearly intimating that this was his thinking: get rid of Hussein. (Readers will remember that during the first Gulf War, his father had resisted the temptation to do this.) As was specified from the outset, the mission began and ended with the removal of the Iraqis from Kuwait.

Subsequently, we imposed a new no-fly zone, which was in place for the following ten years. This alone was an expensive proposition for us, to say nothing of the routine dustups between our pilots and the Iraqis.)

I was also aware that our Air Force was getting tired of policing the no-fly zone, as, I'm sure, was President Bush. He was clearly forming an opinion that his father had made a mistake in not ridding the world of Hussein when he had the chance. I was worried that we were about to undertake an enormous mission just to eliminate one bad guy who may not have been the guilty party in this instance, no matter how horrible he was.

I told the President: "We can't do this. We don't have the capability to get rid of all the bad guys. There are too many bad guys in the world. The only reason to attack him is if his plans include helping terrorists bring more serious attacks against the U.S."

I added the following caveat: "If I come to the conclusion that he really does have weapons of mass destruction or is about to get nuclear weapons that might wind up in the hands of terrorists, then I could be for doing something about him."

Bush replied: "Go out to the CIA — do all of your work, do your investigation — figure out what is what, and then we'll talk."

So that's what I did. I spoke at length to the CIA four or five times — long meetings with all their people. As I recall, they even brought in the opinion of the intelligence service in Europe. And I listened to everything that they all had to say. I asked all the relevant questions you could possibly consider.

And I concluded that Saddam Hussein undoubtedly had weapons of mass destruction, poison gas, chemical weapons, and that he was trying hard and very close to obtaining either a nuclear device or the technology for nuclear weapons.

Afterward, I went back to the White House and told George Bush that I could agree to doing this, but he needed a War Resolution out of Congress. I further advised him to put together a coalition of allies like one that had been formed for Gulf War I.

"I hope you'll go to the U.N. because Saddam Hussein has not complied with all the U.N. resolutions and other things that have been done to rid him of nuclear weapons and weapons of mass destruction." I added.

I reverted to my caucus and told them that I was going to sponsor the resolution to take out Saddam Hussein and to go to war with Iraq. It was one of the most difficult caucuses I ever held. As you can imagine, many Democrats were adamantly opposed to all of this.

I told the caucus, "Look, this is my decision. I've done my own investigation. You should do your own. I'm not going to tell anybody how to vote on this. This is one of the biggest decisions you'll make in your public service. This is why we're here — to make these kinds of decisions.

"Everybody has to decide on what's best for the people that sent you here as their representative."

We argued the case on the floor. Most Democrats voted against the resolution, but a significant minority voted for it. I voted for it. The Republicans backed it. It passed into law on October 16, 2002.

And then it was off to war, a second time, with Iraq.

The timing was coincident to the mid-term elections, and — as best I could given all that was going on — I kept my sights on winning back the House for the Democrats.

I traveled the country relentlessly raising money and recruiting candidates. There was a lot of optimism across the party (including among the candidates that I recruited).

In an election fundraising cycle that shattered previous records (but is positively quaint compared to the fourteen billion dollars generated in 2020), we raised $220 million — a figure that still badly lagged the Republican tally of just over $400 million. This involved a combination of pressing on our major donor sources to dig even deeper into their wallets, along with a big grass roots effort.

These efforts notwithstanding, Election Night was a disappointment for us. The Republicans actually gained eight seats in the House, and, in addition, flipped the Senate in their favor—the first time in history where a mid-term election had resulted in a first-term president's party gaining control of a branch of Congress.

In retrospect, it's clear that 9/11 and the unfolding new war blotted out all other issues to our significant electoral disadvantage.

Before we launched the war in earnest, Bush did try to get the U.N. involved. He went there himself and sent Secretary of State Colin Powell to make our case, but they just couldn't get cooperation from other countries. Instead, the United Kingdom, Australia, Spain, and Poland joined us in what was dubbed the "Coalition of the Willing."

But this was a poor substitute for the type of U.N. Resolution that backed Gulf War I. As all of this was unfolding, I called Secretary Powell and said:

"Mr. Secretary, surely, we're not going to do this unless we get the U.N. with us." And he said: "Dick, I totally agree. I don't think we should unless we can get the U.N. It would be a very big problem."

All of this was very embarrassing for him. As he later testified before Congress, he had accepted the same information upon which I based my own decision.

And we were wrong.

We invaded Iraq, and, after a thorough search of locations where we expected to find weapons of mass destruction, chemical weapons, the beginnings of nuclear weapons, or nuclear components, we came up empty.

I've often wondered why and where we went wrong. My conclusion runs contrary to a popular narrative that Bush had fabricated the whole threat. I do not believe that. He was, however, deeply prodded by Deputy Secretary of Defense Paul Wolfowitz, who went on to become President of the World Bank.

At that time, however, Wolfowitz aggressively advanced the theory (which, in fairness, makes some sense) that unless we intervened in these Middle Eastern countries which were producing these terrorists, we were never going to be free from terrorism and the danger of attacks like 9/11. We therefore had no alternative other than to rid the world of these horrible regimes whether they be in Iraq, Syria, or elsewhere.

It was an idealistic viewpoint but entirely impractical. Our post "Mission Accomplished" occupation of Iraq dragged on and carried forward, in that country and others, to this day. As we are now learning after twenty hard, bloody years in Afghanistan, our withdrawal simply eases the way for groups such as the Taliban to return to their bloody ways. This same story has been unfolding for many centuries.

During that time, people would routinely ask me how long we were going to remain in Iraq. And I'd say: "Well, we've been in Germany and Japan for seventy years. You tell me how long we're going to be in Iraq." And that's kind of the way it worked out.

Seventy years ago, a small group of people could not inflict the kind of damage that was inflicted on us on 9/11, but that's the nature of the world in which we now reside.

I met with many of the families who lost loved ones on 9/11 in New York, cried with them, heard their stories of how their children were devastated because they lost their father or their mother. I think about them every day. But our tools for response were limited and we needed to use careful judgment.

I'm often asked if I would have voted for the war if I knew then what I know now. The obvious answer is no because the criteria for me was that he had weapons of mass destruction or the raw materials for nuclear weapons. So, obviously, if I had known that to be not true, I would not have voted for the war.

But more than that, I look back on the decision I made and how I made it, and I consider it a highly personal failure. I should have done more exploration, more probing on the question of whether Hussein had weapons of mass destruction.

In retrospect, it's clear that Hussein felt perpetually threatened in the region and spent considerable resources falsely talking up his military capabilities. It was a constant PR effort on his part to convince the world that he had WMDs and would respond in kind if attacked. But it was all a ruse.

Perhaps with more inquiry we could have uncovered the scam. This has been a major source of unhappiness for me. After the war, I visited places like Walter Reed Hospital and saw horribly wounded soldiers — patriots to the core and our heroes. And I cried because I had a major role in sending them into action based upon faulty intelligence.

I will always regret that decision, even though I did my best. I will carry that decision to my grave with deep regret. It was the best decision I knew how to make, but at the time it wasn't good enough. And if I were one of those young people, or a member of their family, I would certainly think that.

So I will never forget that this was a failure of mine and that I did not live up to what I believe public servants should be.

All of which brings us to the 108th Congress, which convened on January 3, 2003. Bush was in the White House, and the Republicans controlled both houses of Congress.

The 108th Congress turned out to be my last rodeo as an elected public servant. How all of that unfolded is the subject of the next chapter.

CHAPTER 11

Reaching for the Sky (Again) and Bidding Farewell

I n the wake of the 2002 Midterm Elections, and our fourth consecutive failure to recapture the House for the Democrats, I knew that I had some important decisions to make and not much time in which to make them. Choices about my career, my leadership role in the House, my role in the direction of the party, and the direction of the country.

The first defining judgment I made was to step down as Minority Leader in the 108th Congress. Instead, I decided to focus my energies on a second run for the Presidency.

The allure of the White House had never left me, my previously described loss in 1988 notwithstanding. Many of my friends and colleagues advised me that winning a presidential election, surviving the primaries, and then taking the General was a numbers game. For most, the odds are very long; but they increase with multiple attempts. I had only tried once so why not give it another go?

As my inclination trended in that direction, the issue of my continuing as the Leader of the Democratic Congressional Caucus came into clearer focus. There was nothing that precluded me from running for the Oval Office as Minority Leader; in fact, the status offered certain unique advantages, particularly in terms of fundraising.

Ironically, however, it was in large part the issue of fundraising that discouraged me against continuing as Minority Leader. As mentioned earlier, I had failed in that role to win back the House for the Democratic Party four consecutive times: '96, '98, '00, and '02. Each cycle, I traveled the country relentlessly to raise that money for the Democratic Congressional Campaign Committee, to challenge in Republican districts, and to defend vulnerable Democrats in in swing regions.

I had spent an inordinate amount of time calling donors and organizers and attending weekend fundraising event all across the country, often accompanied by other members of the Caucus. This was all before the current era where much of the money is raised online. Back then, the development of personal relationships, through face-to-face interaction with donors and fundraising organizers, was the only way to get it done.

However, I believe that political relationship building needs guardrails, and I want to state outright that I am entirely against making legislative promises to donors. I believe this to be anathema to everything I stand for in representative government. And as a result, I did not do it. Instead, I emphasized concepts such as common values and shared visions as to how the country should be governed. In my financing pitches, I conveyed to potential donors my belief that their financial support was an act of patriotic generosity rendered for the cause of good government.

But one way or another, money was essential; you cannot manage a campaign on air. We needed cash — a great deal of it — and this required me yet again to tap the largesse of contributors from earlier cycles. In the four preceding sequences, I had assured these individuals and groups that their assistances would put us over the top; but each time we came up short.

I simply did not feel that I had it in me to reach out a fifth time — essentially with the same story — to the same groups that had funded our efforts over the previous decade.

The other reasons I decided to stand down were more personal. I've always believed that there was, or should be, a calendar limit imposed upon all political leaders. There are times to be in office and to be in a leadership position, and times to withdraw. There are always high-quality young men and women who represent the future. Ultimately, there comes a point when the right thing to do is to step aside and make way for them.

I committed myself to understanding the moment that my time had run its course and to start thinking about doing something else. I had long envisioned myself eventually entering the Private Sector for financial considerations, among other reasons. I made a nice salary during my time in Congress, ultimately earning $150,000 per year. This afforded me a comfortable lifestyle for my family, and I wanted for nothing. But I did wish to leave my children some wealth beyond my Federal pension.

At that point, I was sixty-two and getting older every day. So I began to formulate a plan. I would withdraw from my leadership position and run for president. And if (as was likely) I failed to win the office, it was an ideal time to begin a new journey and learn new things.

I didn't know where this path would lead me, and that was a large part of the appeal. One way or another, I would learn. I would grow. To me, this was a big part of what life was all about.

The first step, though, was to withdraw as Leader — an action I was prepared to take (and in fact did take) at the beginning of the 108th Congress in January 2003. Those around me were not unilaterally pleased with this decision. My staff was disappointed, which was understandable given this associated impact on their careers. Beyond this, however, many of my political contacts urged me to reconsider. They told me I could stay on as Leader and still run for President. In fact they said that my status in the leadership would help with fundraising and other mission-critical aspects of a presidential campaign.

I rejected these arguments out of hand. I didn't want to solicit the same donors that had supported our previous four efforts, and beyond that, I didn't want to dilute the fundraising resources of the Democratic Congressional Caucus or their candidate recruitment activities.

I simply did not believe that I should stay in this job and run for president simultaneously. It was one or the other. And I felt the pressure of time. The sooner I resigned the Leadership, the better I would serve my Party, that could then elect leaders in an orderly fashion. In turn, the new Leadership could then focus all its efforts and energies on overseeing the legislative process and best positioning the Democrats for 2004. The House Democrats selected Nance Pelosi to succeed me, and she became the first female Speaker of the House in US history. And in my opinion she became the best Speaker in the history of the House.

Once I announced this decision, I reverted to a role in which I was entirely comfortable, a congressman representing my district and the country to the best of my ability. Beyond this, however, I faced the formal decision as to whether to run for the Democratic nomination for president in 2004.

There were a number of reasons I believed that the timing to do so was favorable. I did not feel at the time that President George W. Bush had amassed a particularly strong track record. Despite this, his poll numbers were still high — ostensibly due to the country's continued coalescence after 9/11. Another contributor may have been favorable views from the electorate associated with our early successes in Gulf War II.

I felt that his popularity levels were artificially high and that he was vulnerable. In addition, I believed that if I ever wanted to make another run, 2004 would be my last opportunity to do so. I had retained many relationships in the critical early nomination states of Iowa and a stronger nationwide network than ever before.

In terms of name recognition, fundraising resources, and political network, I believed that I had an edge over others that might enter the field. Recall that in 1988 I'd only raised twelve million dollars. That this was certainly a key factor in my undoing.

I thought that this time, surely, would be different. I had spent the better part of the previous decade fundraising. I knew the game, the playing field, and the rules of engagement. I could identify the right constituents to solicit — not for political quid pro quo — but rather those with the desire and resources to financially support Democratic values. And to beat George W. Bush in 2004.

I also felt very strongly, particularly at the time, that the next president should be someone with congressional experience. For most of my adult life we had biased toward tapping those with Executive Branch credentials. After the two terms — started by Kennedy and ended by Johnson and followed by Nixon (each of whom served in Both the Senate and House) —we displayed a preference for Governors. First Carter, then Reagan, another Vice President (George H.W. Bush), then Clinton from Arkansas, and after that, the then-sitting president, former Texas Governor George W. Bush. Thus, for a nearly a generation (1981 to 2003), the only White House occupant that had spent time in Congress was the first George H.W. Bush, who represented Texas in the House of Representatives in the late '60s.

While not explicitly essential, I believed that a president who spent his career in Congress would work better with those legislative bodies and get more accomplished.

At any rate, all roads were leading me toward another run. As is natural and appropriate, one of my first areas of focus was to scan and evaluate the field of potential competitors for the nomination.

John Kerry had the highest profile of my potential competitors having served in Vietnam, worked as Lieutenant Governor of Massachusetts under Michael Dukakis, and was in the midst of his third term as Senator. Then there was Vermont Governor Howard Dean and North Carolina Senator John Edwards. The race also included Reverend Al Sharpton, General Wesley Clark, former Illinois Senator Carol Mosely Braun, Connecticut Senator Joe Lieberman, and former Cleveland Mayor Dennis Kucinich.

Dean and Kucinich came from party's far left, and it was my hope that they would divide the support from that constituency. Overall, I liked my chances against the field. Again, in 1988, I had a great deal of support in Iowa and New Hampshire where I had spent an inordinate amount of time going door to door. I believed this was the main reason I won the former state and came in second in the latter.

I believed these relationships were still intact, which I thought enabled me to spend less time on the ground in those states and more time on the phone fundraising.

For a time, this appeared to work. Late in 2003, I was well ahead in the Iowa polls, and everyone thought I stood a great chance to win the nomination. But it was a big field and the primaries were still weeks away. Longstanding political strategy dictates that as the frontrunner, the one mistake you must avoid at all costs is engaging in direct conflict with the candidate immediately behind you in the polls. At the time, my closest challenger was Howard Dean, and I tried my best to give him a wide berth. But he took the opposite tack. He ran saturation ads showing me in the Rose Garden with George Bush announcing my support of Gulf War II — an anathema to a significant portion of the Democratic base.

These messages struck home. Within a week, my Iowa lead had evaporated; I went from first to fourth or fifth.

At that point, I knew I was in big trouble and knew that I had to respond to Dean. I ran some adds about his stance on Medicare, which caused his standing in the polls to plummet.

And, as is consistent with the playbook, when Number 1 and Number 2 begin to battle one another, another candidate steals Center Stage.

That candidate was John Kerry, who catapulted from the middle of the field and finished first. I came in fourth, behind Kerry, Edwards, and Howard Dean, who continued on to other primary contests but ultimately dropped out.

Kerry went on to win New Hampshire, adjacent to his home state of Massachusetts and shortly thereafter sealed the nomination. No other candidate seriously challenged him.

But it was all over for me after Iowa. I decided that night to withdraw. I conceded the night of the Caucus, taking care to thank many great people who had helped me along the way. My campaign manager, Steve Murphy; Bill Carrick, who ran my media campaign; and David Plouffe, who went on to fame and fortune with the Obama's Election — all did a great job managing my campaign. My loyal and talented friend, Joyce Aboussie, did her usual awesome work. But the vote for the war in Iraq sealed had my fate.

After that there was extensive speculation that Kerry would select me as his running mate, so much so that in early June 2004, a few days before the Convention, the New York Post ran a front page that I was to be on the ticket.

Instead, Kerry picked John Edwards and ultimately lost a close General Election.

George Bush had won a second term.

So, after twenty-eight years of representing my district, the State of Missouri, and the nation, I stepped down from my seat in the House. It was a good time to move on. After fourteen Congressional terms, serving under five presidents, I had dealt with an unimaginably wide array of issues — budgetary matters, health-care reform, international and domestic terrorism, two wars, impeachment, public health, and safety. I had risen to the leadership of my party's caucus in the United States House of Representatives. I had seen it all, done it all. Most importantly, I had met the American people in Missouri and across the country. I was then, and still am, in awe of their "goodness." I will forever hold a positive view of the American people and their ability to manage a country — of, by, and for the people.

But my time was over. The moment had come to move on.

There is much to reflect on the experience, including the joys and disappointments I had experienced, the impact on the path of the nation, and where I believe matters stand now.

I left with much gratitude for the honor to serve and almost no regrets. At the end of the day, for me, it was about the divine wisdom of the process — the system our founders had gifted to us. I felt at the time, and still believe today, that we must guard it with everything inside us.

Perhaps there are some grand messages to draw from one man's journey down this road, through those halls. Perhaps not. I'll leave the reader to decide.

I will do my best to summarize my perspectives on all of this in the next and final chapter.

CHAPTER 12

535 Not 1

So, what's it all about?

I wrote this book because I wanted to give readers a better understanding of what it was like to be a member of a group of five hundred and thirty-five people who are charged with the responsibility of making important decisions for three hundred and fifty million fellow citizens.

Further, I hope this story has afforded the reader a better understanding of how difficult, cumbersome, and time-consuming that decision-making process can be, and, by obvious comparison, how much more simply (and destructively) those decisions could be reached by one, single, controlling human being.

The stories contained throughout are just a vehicle to convey my strong belief in the value of democracy over autocracy in human governance. In most human organizations based on outcomes, bottom-up decision making is infinitely superior to the top-down processes — the military being perhaps the most obvious exception.

In my twenty-eight years of public service, I saw and participated in the final resolution of many very controversial, bitterly debated issues. I witnessed many occasions where the losing contingent willingly, if grudgingly, accepted the decision of Congress even though they were deeply disappointed in the outcome.

The reason they did so was that they thought the process had been fair. They had had their chance to make the arguments for their position. They got to vote on their issues, thereby representing millions of Americans that held their view. But their position lost — in a fairly conducted canvas of five hundred and thirty-five stewards of the public trust (representative of over 300 million Americans).

I also hope the reader obtained some insight into the complexities of compromise, which, in addition to leading to the practical outcomes that form our governance, can offer vital assistance in helping legislators understand the viewpoints of others. When this happens, even the losers of a given legislative argument stand to gain important perspectives.

Contrast this with a process under which one, or a small group, of unaccountable individuals make critical decisions. The losers in any given debate are left with little except justifiable anger and outrage.

In our democratic republic, everyone can justifiably celebrate the process. As Winston Churchill, in 1947, famously described it to the House of Commons:

"Many forms of Government have been tried and will be tried in this world of sin and woe. No one pretends that democracy is perfect or all-wise. Indeed, it has been said that democracy is the worst form of Government except for all those other forms that have been tried from time to time. . ."

I would put it a little bit differently. To me, the magic in the process is embodied in the concept of self-governance and in my belief that government works best when it is conducted by the "consent of the governed." This 240-year-old, successful American experiment is the best roadmap for the majesty of Democracy in the history of the world. The alternative, as discussed throughout, is the authoritarian model under which the ruling person or class must ultimately use violence, or effective threats to enforce their decisions.

That is the way countries such as China, Russia, and others are run today. Our founders rejected this approach with then radical ideas that were articulated in our founding documents. When Benjamin Franklin, upon departing Independence Hall in Philadelphia in 1787 — after the ratification of the Constitution — was asked what kind of government we have, he replied "We have a republic, if you can keep it."

We still have a republic. If we can keep it. And keeping it has been our challenge for 240 years. It remains so today.

Doing so, I believe, requires citizens to prioritize the election process over any policy goals. Individuals and groups may be passionately invested in specific policies, but if their advocacy comes at the expense of destroying the election process, the whole system will collapse.

I believe that prioritizing policy goals over a valid election process and the peaceful transition of power would be at best transiently appealing, and at worst, ultimately lead to horrible outcomes. Policy goals and viewpoints change with time and conditions. But once an autocrat construct replaces a republic, it becomes difficult or impossible to restore the agency of the electorate.

To reinforce the point, I quote from American Schism, a recently published book by Seth David Radwell, a business executive turned full-time author. The book traces the historical origins of the types of conflicts described herein. In offering up his vision for a way forward, states:

"The Enlightenment point of view can be expressed as follows: Government derives its authority as a form of social contract created by, subscribed to and for the benefit of the people. By agreeing to form a self-governing society, citizens abide by a system of law and order supported by a framework comprising a balance of powers in order to maximize the well-being of all the common good."

Further on he draws inspiration from Harvard Professor Danielle Allen: "The notion of political equality, the idea that every American should play an active role in the workings of our democracy is fundamental." Allen insists that for a democracy — a government of the people — to work, the populace must fully embrace and even cherish democracy as a process. It must be strong enough to overcome the pain and conflict that its practice evokes.

So, what are the most important threats to our ability to keep our republic? My opinions are as follows.

The first and most important threat is the extreme division and polarization of the American people, which is arguably at its highest point in at least two generations. In 1858, in Springfield, Illinois, accepting the Republican nomination for Senate, Abraham Lincoln famously said, "A house divided against itself cannot stand." And we all know what happened after that.

It seems the divisions among the American people today are reminiscent of those we experienced before the Civil War. And when we question why Congress today is dysfunctional — facing significant difficulty in making any decisions at all — it is directly attributed to the bitter disagreements among the people. Congress, by necessity, reflects the attitude of the constituents it represents. If the people are deeply divided, Congress will be deeply divided.

Putting aside the Civil War, we have experienced other periods of bitter divisions among our people. Reconstruction after the war ended, the Great Depression of the 1930s, the Vietnam War, and the continuing struggles for civil rights all come to mind.

Are the American people more divided in these prior times other than the Civil War? I believe we are. And I believe the reason for that is the gradual destruction of a healthy information environment in the country. All forms of governance in human history have relied extensively on information flows in the management of their affairs. Authoritarian regimes have always used propaganda and manipulation of information to keep control of their population. By contrast, in democracies, all political players work authentically to use free-flowing information forums to burnish their image and the wisdom of their ideas, as well as (it must be said) to disparage their opponents and their policies.

Central to the process is Freedom of Speech and the Press, which has been enshrined in our Constitution. Unlike the authoritarian model, most democracies have insisted on a free press not dominated by any side in the political fray as an essential to having a successful democracy.

Freedom of press is enshrined in the First Amendment of the Constitution for two hundred and thirty years. Freedom of the Press has always been the secret sauce of American democracy. Free government and free markets are built on individual decision making. A free press provides the information we need to make sound political, business, and individual decisions.

In 1787, while serving as Minister to France, Thomas Jefferson wrote to Revolutionary War hero Edward Carrington:

"The basis of our governments being the opinion of the people, the very first object should be to keep that right; and were it left to me to decide whether we should have a government without newspapers or newspapers without a government, I should not hesitate a moment to prefer the latter. But I should mean that every man should receive those papers & be capable of reading them."

The sentiment has endured, but throughout our history we have justifiably worried about the information gatekeepers being corrupted and dominated by a particular political party or cause. In recent years, cable TV channels have become increasingly slanted by both political sides. Political parties have always sought to take over newspapers, radio and TV stations, and now cable outlets, but they had never succeeded the way they have today. And now, in addition, with every human on Earth having the ability through social media to act as a de facto media outlet, and to speak without filter, it is increasingly difficult to see how we can have a healthy information culture.

In addition, some of the internet media platforms have a business plan that uses industrial scale data extraction algorithms along with algorithms to process information to people that will make them angry, anxious, and keep their attention for hours at a time. That attention yields greater revenue to the platform. In short, attention-surveillance capitalism may not be compatible with having a successful democracy.

If many citizens wind up marinating for hours a day in an alternative reality that nurtures confirmation bias and never considers counter facts or counter views, the result is bitter division and polarization.

The phenomenon is now global in nature. Indisputably, domestic parties with nefarious objectives and foreign adversaries are accessing our platforms to conduct a form of information warfare. It is dividing the American people. Their goal is to divide the American people, break their trust in any source of information, and weaken or destroy America.

In my view, these developments pose the most critical threat to the survival of our democracy in my lifetime. If citizens in a democracy cannot get access to valid, objective information, they cannot make good decisions. There are no longer shared facts.

Due to the veritable onslaught of unfiltered streams of opinion, there is a dearth of shared facts and consensus as to what is real and what is engineered and agenda driven. Citizens are bombarded with truths, untruths, and everything in between. They do not, cannot, know who or what to believe. There is no trust in any information.

There is no easy or clear way to remedy this problem. Regulation is necessary, but the bitter division among the people, and therefore within Congress, makes identifying a compromise on this problem unlikely at best and impossible at worst. Perhaps citizen and advertising pressure can be used to get the social media platforms to reform their algorithmic behavior — to even be rewarded for changing their system so it encourages people to encounter counter facts and views. Also, to construct ways citizens can come together to hear one another's views and see if consensus on controversial issues can be achieved. This could be creativity for the whole country — similar to what my Leadership meetings achieved when I put 60 people in a room every night for two hours.

Audrey Tang, Digital Minister of Taiwan, has created an innovative communication system on the internet for the Taiwanese government. It offers an opportunity for citizens to engage in an open forum where various views on controversial issues can be heard in working towards consensus.

We must determine how to use the amazing technology that has contributed to democratic change in many countries to now be a force for promoting a healthy information environment instead of promoting polarization and disunity.

To say it again: a house divided against itself cannot stand.

But if our 240-year-old process of collaboration, patient listening, and compromise cannot solve this, our democracy might be doomed. In the meantime, we must remain optimistic that sensible regulations in this area can solve this problem without compromising freedom of speech. We must have freedom of speech. I don't believe we can survive without it.

As to what remains of the free press, I hold out hope that many of our young citizens will seek journalism training so that they can carry on the proud tradition of acting as arbiters of information flows. Ironically, the political interests that use all the various media outlets for their political advantage — thereby helping to sow more division and polarization — are hastening the day when the holy and essential power of media will seek to exist. There will no longer be healthy political competition. The winners will simply control content to their own (perceived) advantage.

But an informed, competent press is not a comprehensive solution. In addition, I believe we must always encourage the citizenry to be responsible consumers of content. Without such a commitment by the general populous, our system of self-government will come under repeated attack.

A third threat comes from the recent efforts of many in the Republican Party to impede election processes, perhaps because they fear they can't compete on a level playing field. But that concern diverges from the rhetoric they employ, which focuses on purported fraud emanating from the other side. To counteract this, they have sponsored significant and varying legislative efforts to add difficulty to the voting process and to allow state agencies to override electoral tallies.

This really amounts to the modern Republican Party giving up on a valid electoral process "by and for the people," and, therefore, giving up on democracy itself. The only solution I see to this problem is that a sufficient portion of the Republican party band together to oppose these practices and make it clear they will always choose country over party.

That is what various Republican election officials did after the 2020 election, even standing up to pleas by President Trump to magically find a few thousand more votes for him and reverse what was otherwise a clear outcome in the presidential election. Former Vice President Mike Pence, who resisted the pleas of President Trump to refuse to recognize the vote outcome in some swing states so that he would be re-elected by fiat, comes to mind. As do Liz Cheney (Republican, Wyoming) and Adam Kinzinger (Republican, Illinois) voting — along with just ten other Republican House members — to recognize the election of President Biden in the face of incredible pushback from President Trump and his followers. Pence, Cheney, Kinzinger, and the ten other Republicans are modern profiles in courage. They put country over party and self!

If either political party takes the extreme tack, our democracy is over and may never return. We must deeply admire the political and personal bravery shown by these Republicans after the 2020 election. There is no solution to this threat other than the individual courage of people like them acting in the spirit of Ben Franklin's "we have a republic if we can keep it."

In the wake of 2020 election, enough Republicans had the grit and courage to keep it. A handful of state and local election officials in Georgia, Arizona and Michigan withstood incredible pressure from President Trump to defend our democratic electoral process.

A fourth threat is the loss of faith by the electorate that their public servants are only there for them and not special interests. If citizens of this nation become convinced that office holders are owned and controlled by the financial campaign contributions of special interests instead of the public as a whole, the system becomes unsustainable. This has always been a threat. But when I came into politics, there was not nearly the amount of campaign money that there is today. In my first campaign for Congress in 1976, I spent the grand total of $70,000 for both a difficult primary campaign and a very tough general election.

The cost of the 2020 Congressional campaign is estimated to be a record $8.7 billion: (https://www.opensecrets.org/news/2021/02/2020-cycle-cost-14p4billion-doubling-16/) .

With all 435 House and 33 Senate seats having been contested, this equates to more than $18 million per election.

One critical implication of this is that there is no way for average citizens — without enormous wealth of their own or easy access to massive donor flows — to be elected to Congress. There is no easy solution to this one either. In an infamous, landmark 2010 decision commonly referred to as "Citizens United," the Supreme Court ruled that money equals speech, rendering it unlawful for Congress to place limits on campaign finance and associated expenditures. As a result, the election process has devolved into an omnivorous money machine, which can only grow in magnitude and influence over time. The 2020 cash grab was more than double the gargantuan amounts raised and spent in 2016. Does anyone think that this trend can do anything but continue?

I believe there is an elegant solution to this problem, and one for which I have developed a particular passion of late. It involves allowing candidates to agree to funding that comes only from individuals, with a cap on how much an individual can contribute. The Federal Government would match these donations, dollar-for-dollar. Candidates who accepted this restriction would know that their opponents could refuse this option and instead access PAC, Super PAC, and unlimited funds they could obtain.

This plan is far from perfect. It wouldn't necessarily level the playing field. Presumably, huge disparities in fundraising in particular races would continue to materialize, and the effectiveness of on-line solicitations of finite amounts would assume a particular prominence. But it would certainly move the dynamic toward one where candidates would be empowered to argue that they seek to represent all the people — not the special interests. As such, they would enable the public to discern more authentically who among their choices was best suited to represent them.

The last threat is the increasing unwillingness of representatives to listen to other members and try to reach compromises that may threaten their re-election viability. When I was Leader, I often had to ask members to vote for very controversial legislation that was good for the country, but contained a lot of political danger for anyone voting for it. I have covered several of these situations earlier in the book.

Often in these cases members would inform me that they agreed with a given policy, but couldn't vote for it due to the negative political implications. And I asked them: "Why did you come here? Did you come here just to have this job or did you come here to make the country better? Did you come here to be about things that are bigger than you?"

I would then typically say: "You know, you don't have to worry about not being re-elected if you would go home and go door-to-door like I did and explain your votes to the people. More often than not they'll give you a fair hearing, will probably still vote for you because they know you, know your motives are good, and that you're really trying to do the right thing for all the people."

Some were willing to do that. Many were not.

So, this problem — the conflicting interests of sound policy and political expediency — abides, and I think it is getting worse because of the polarization of the American people and their single-minded commitment to certain issues. The prevailing attitude of many among the politically active is that they only want what they want, and they are not inclined to vote for a member of Congress who is willing to compromise.

In the end, our challenge is to elect individuals willing to put country over self. Over the course of my public service career, I believe I tried to do just that — sometimes successfully, sometimes less so. Others mentioned in this book did so magnificently, while still others took the opposite approach — much, I believe, to our detriment.

In total, 535 individuals managing the public affairs of over three hundred million citizens was, is, and always will be a daunting but worthwhile challenge. We have a republic — let's strive to keep it. We can do this, but only with great effort and focus. If we succeed, we will continue to thrive. If not, then Abraham Lincoln's warning of government of the people, by the people, and for the people perishing from this earth may become a reality.

It's up to us — one nation, 535 representatives, and citizens numbering in the hundreds of millions. The future is in our hands. It always has been.

Our magnificent governmental structure created ten generations ago by our founders is a legacy that we must preserve above all other considerations. Let's agree to use this divine gift as wisely as we are able, lest we allow it to slip through our fingers and into the oblivion of tyranny.